LEFT-HANDED
BANJO SCALES
INFINITY

Master the Universe of Scales In Every Style and Genre

ANDY SCHNEIDER

SEEING MUSIC
METHOD BOOKS

CONTENTS

INFINITY IS IN YOUR MIND
7

FRETBOARD DIAGRAMS
9

HOW TO READ FRETBOARD DIAGRAMS   9
WHAT ABOUT THE 5TH STRING?   11
A NOTE ABOUT FRETBOARD DIAGRAMS   11

MAJOR SCALES, TRIADS AND CHORDS
13

IT ALL STARTS WITH A SCALE   13
HOW MAJOR SCALES ARE BUILT   14
MAJOR TRIADS   16
MAJOR CHORDS   16
G MAJOR SCALE, TRIAD AND CHORD   17

HOW TO USE THIS BOOK
19

SPELLING   19
COMMON STYLE AND GENRE USE   19
CHORD FAMILY   20
SCALE SUBSTITUTIONS   20
SCALES   21
EXERCISES   22

MODES AND MODAL THEORY
25

WHAT ARE MODES?   25
HOW ARE MODES USED?   27

IONIAN 31
OVERVIEW 31
SCALES 33
EXERCISES 34

DORIAN 37
OVERVIEW 37
SCALES 39
EXERCISES 40

PHRYGIAN 43
OVERVIEW 43
SCALES 45
EXERCISES 46

LYDIAN 49
OVERVIEW 49
SCALES 51
EXERCISES 52

MIXOLYDIAN 55
OVERVIEW 55
SCALES 57
EXERCISES 58

AEOLIAN 61
OVERVIEW 61
SCALES 63
EXERCISES 64

LOCRIAN 67
OVERVIEW 67
SCALES 69
EXERCISES 70

MAJOR PENTATONIC 73
OVERVIEW 73
SCALES 75
EXERCISES 76

MINOR PENTATONIC 79
OVERVIEW 79
SCALES 81
EXERCISES 82

BLUES SCALE 85
OVERVIEW 85
SCALES 87
EXERCISES 88

WHOLE TONE 91
OVERVIEW 91
SCALES 93
EXERCISES 94

HALF/WHOLE DIMINISHED 97
OVERVIEW 97
SCALES 99
EXERCISES 100

MELODIC MINOR 105
OVERVIEW *105*
SCALES *108*
EXERCISES *110*

HARMONIC MINOR 115
OVERVIEW *115*
SCALES *117*
EXERCISES *118*

CHROMATIC 121
OVERVIEW *121*
SCALES *123*

YOU'VE EXPLORED THE UNIVERSE 125

CHORD AND MODE REFERENCE 126

SEEING MUSIC
METHOD BOOKS

LEFT-HANDED
BANJO SCALES
INFINITY

INFINITY IS IN YOUR MIND

||||||||||||||||||||||||||||||||||||||||||||||||||||||||||||||||||||||||||||||||

ACROSS THE UNIVERSE

In a real sense, music is its own universe. There are worlds of sounds, styles and tones that exist in a seemingly countless array of flavors. Just as the world was once thought flat and the sky a mere mural, discoveries were made - boundaries moved. With each seeker exploring at the edge of the known, new possibilities were realized. The known universe became so large, humankind had to acknowledge that it only knew of the known universe - that there must be more left to discover. More that would be discovered.

This is how it is with music, as well. Scales are the foundation of nearly all music. This book exists to show you some of their vast possibilities and point you toward making discoveries of your own.

||||||||||||||||||||||||||||||||||||||||||||||||||||||||||||||||||||||||||||||||

In my years teaching instrumental music and talking with other professional string players, I've noticed that we all have developed an ability to "see" the music we play on the fretboard of the instrument. We see the music we play as a simple relationship of shapes and relative positions. Look at these two shapes:

Just as you recognize the shapes above, stringed instrumentalists see music on the fretboard of their instrument. This is an inherently special gift we who play stringed instruments have been given. No other kind of instrument makes it so easy for the musician to have a visual roadmap of the music, making things like improvisation or transposing a song to another key so easy. Our fingers follow these maps to get to the music. This book will show you how to see music as simple shapes and use these shapes to more quickly and proficiently play and create music.

We'll be covering how music is constructed and 'looks' on the neck of the banjo. While we won't get too far into any particular musical style or specific techniques, the information here is common to all Western music: Rock, Folk, Country, Pop, Classical, and Jazz. While the first steps of banjo playing are the same for everyone, the next few steps of learning scales can be taught many different ways. I'm going to walk you through what I believe is the fastest and most powerful way. Learning banjo scales with a visual method makes it so much easier and minimizes memorization. You will develop life-long skills that you will use every day you pick up a banjo.

One of the best things about making music is that the only limitations are in the mind of the musician making the music. While banjo is typically considered a Bluegrass, Country or Folk instrument, there's absolutely no reason it couldn't be used in a Jazz setting. Or old-time Rock and Roll. Or even Heavy Metal! Whether you're a traditional instrumentalist or you have ideas about making new music the world has never heard before, you'll be able to apply the concepts and skills you'll learn inside this book. I look forward to hearing a world filled with your music!

Turn the page, you're about to "see" music!

-Andy Schneider

FRETBOARD DIAGRAMS

HOW TO READ FRETBOARD DIAGRAMS

You're ready to start learning scales. The diagrams in this book are kind of like pictures of what you'll see when you look at your banjo. These diagrams will apply to both 4- and 5-string banjos.

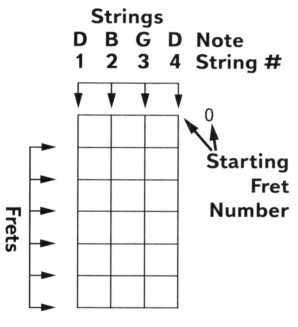

FIG.1 - FRET NOTATION

FIG.2 - FRETBOARD

Hold your banjo upright in front of you and look at fretboard. The strings run up and down, the frets run horizontally. That is the view used in fretboard diagrams.

Let's try playing our first note. As indicated in Figure 3, play open D, the 4th string. An open circle indicates an open string, one that is played without fretting with the right hand.

With your picking hand, feel free to use a pick, thumb or fingers. For now, do whatever is comfortable.

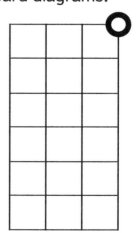

FIG.3 - OPEN 4TH STRING

FRETBOARD DIAGRAMS 9

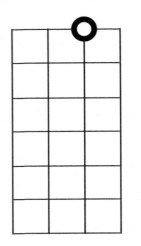

0

FIG.4 - OPEN 3RD STRING

Did that go well? Try another, this time open G, the 3rd string.

Figure 5 tells you to play the note found at the black dot on the 3rd String at the 3rd fret. It's the 3rd fret because it's three fret higher up the neck than the "0" in the upper right corner of the diagram. The zero indicates that the diagram begins at the nut or "zeroth" fret.

The "2" next to the black dot indicates you'll use your first finger of your fretting hand as in Figure 6.

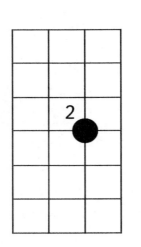

0

FIG.5 - FRET NOTATION

FIG.6 - RIGHT-HAND FINGERING

On these diagrams, a filled in circle indicates that you'll put your finger at that fret. Actually, you'll put your finger just behind the fret, not right on top of the fret. The fret, not your finger, is what stops the vibration of the string and changes its length.

Keeping your finger pressed with medium pressure, just behind the fret will produce the clearest and best sound.

Don't confuse a fretboard diagram with a musical staff. Music staves indicate pitch and rhythm. Fretboard diagrams like Figure 5 are like a roadmap, showing you where to place your fingers.

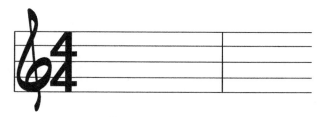

FIG.7 - MUSICAL STAFF

WHAT ABOUT THE 5TH STRING?

Some banjos have 4 strings, others have 5. The 5th string is typically used as a *drone*. That is, it is often plucked but rarely are notes fretted on it. Additionally, the notes there are exactly the same as the notes on the 1st string. In other words, when playing a scale on the banjo, players will typically access the notes on the 1st string, although they could just as well play those notes on the same fret of the 5th string. *Enharmonically*, they are the same.

Since visuallizing scales across strings 1-4 is fairly easy, for now focus on scales that just use those strings. When you encounter a note on the 1st string at the 5th fret or higher, you can experiment by playing that note on the same fret of the 5th string. You'll find that it is the same note.

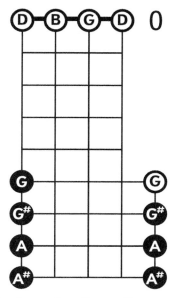

FIG.8 - 1ST VS 5TH STRING NOTES

A NOTE ABOUT FRETBOARD DIAGRAMS

Most other books place the dot in-between the fret lines. This kind of diagram is helpful for getting quick answers about where fretting fingers belong, but this book also demonstrates the reason *why* notes are placed where they are. Understanding the "why" of music actually makes it easier to learn and memorize. You'll start to make associations about chords and scales that will amplify your learning.

When you see a dot in this book, you'll know that it is showing you the note to be played and that you'll place your finger just behind that fret to hear it.

SOUNDCHECK

Fretboard diagrams indicate where to find a note and what finger to use to play it.

The number in the upper-right corner of a fretboard diagram indicates on which fret the diagram begins.

Fretboard diagrams should not be confused with musical staves.

SEEING MUSIC
METHOD BOOKS

MAJOR SCALES, TRIADS AND CHORDS

|||||||||||||||||||||||||||||||||||||||||||||||||||||||||||||||||||||||||||

THE NUTS AND BOLTS

Know the simple but powerful relationship between scales, triads and chords. Learn to play Major scales.

|||||||||||||||||||||||||||||||||||||||||||||||||||||||||||||||||||||||||||

IT ALL STARTS WITH A SCALE

Scales are awesome because ALL music comes from them! First, all melodies come from scales. But perhaps even more important: scales, triads and chords are all related. Scales produce triads, triads produce chords.

Scales → Triads → Chords

FIG.9 - SCALES PRODUCE TRIADS, TRIADS PRODUCE CHORDS

The C Major Scale

Take a look at the C Major scale. The notes of the C Major scale in order are C, D, E, F, G, A, B and C.

CDEFGABC

FIG.10 - C MAJOR SCALE NOTE NAMES

All the notes here are separated by a whole-step, except those indicated by the "^" symbol. Those are separated by a half-step. On the banjo, two notes that are one fret apart are separated by a half-step. Two half-steps equals one whole step, which would be two frets distance.

Again, most notes here are one whole-step apart, with the exception being those separated by a half-step.

In Figure 11, start on the 4th string, 10th fret and place your 2nd finger there. It's indicated by the dot with the "X" through it. This is the root, C.

Play the C, then keeping your 2nd finger there, add your 4th finger at the 12th fret on the same string. Play this note, D.

Now, you can release these notes. On the 3rd string at the 9th fret, place your first finger. Play this E.

Next play F, then G, then on to the 2nd string, similarly. At the end, you'll reach the high C.

The finger you should use for each fret is indicated in Figure 11.

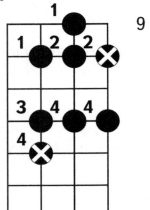

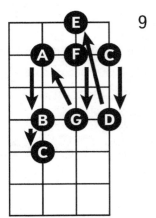

FIG.11 - C MAJOR SCALE WITH FINGERINGS   FIG.12 - C MAJOR SCALE WITH NOTE NAMES

HOW MAJOR SCALES ARE BUILT

A major scale is a particular series of whole and half-steps.

A half-step is the distance between two notes that are one fret apart. A whole-step is equal to two half-steps.

In all major scales, the half-steps are between the 3rd and 4th notes (or *degrees*) and the 7th and root degrees. All the other notes are a whole step apart, or the equivalent of two frets in distance from each other.

In the C Major scale, the half-steps are between E and F and between B and C. Take note of them in Figures 11 and 12.

MEMORY SUPERPOWER

To easily remember the fingering of the C Major scale, use this tip:

On the 4th string, you use fingers 2 and 4. Next, on the 3rd string, you use fingers 1, 2 and 4 and on the 2nd string, you use 1, 3 and 4.

When you say it to yourself a few times, it even starts to sound kind of musical. Say, "2 4, 1 2 4, 1 3 4."

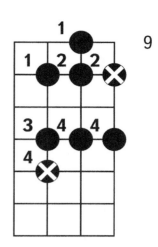

FIG.13 - C MAJOR SCALE

Remember how some notes can be found in several places on the banjo? Here's another example.

C Major Down the Neck

Have a look at Figure 14, then Figure 15. They are two different ways to play a C Major scale.

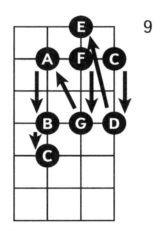

FIG.14 - C MAJOR SCALE STARTING ON 4TH STRING

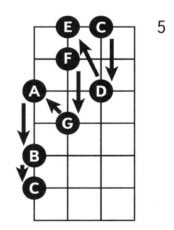

FIG.15 - C MAJOR SCALE STARTING ON 3RD STRING

Do you see how the notes are arranged in the same order on each of the three strings? On the left, the 4th string uses two notes, C and D. On the right, the 3rd string uses two notes, C and D. The following strings also follow a pattern of E, F and G. Then A, B and C.

PLAY C MAJOR MID-NECK

In Figure 15, you'll start by playing C on the 3rd string at the 5th fret with your 1st finger.

Play the scale in Figure 15. Now play the scale from Figure 14. They sound alike, don't they?

SEEING MUSIC

Although they are a little obtuse, if you spotted the similarity of the shapes of Figures 14 and 15, then you are already beginning to "see" music on the banjo!

MAJOR TRIADS

A triad is a collection of three notes of a scale. Triads are worth studying because they are the building blocks of chords. Scales produce triads, triads produce chords. Have a look.

Each note of a scale, can be given a number name, or degree. Using C Major as an example: C, D, E, F, G, A, B and C have scale degrees 1, 2, 3, 4, 5, 6, 7 and 1, again. While the last note, C, is the 8th note, it's still called the 1st degree, because although it's one octave higher, its still the same note name, as the 1st degree, or root of the scale.

A triad contains the 1st, 3rd and 5th degrees of the scale. So a C Major triad is spelled C, E, G.

PLAY A TRIAD

C, E and G are the 1st, 3rd and 5th degrees of the C Major scale. One at a time, play these three notes: C, then E, then G in Figure 16.

It has a familiar sound, doesn't it?

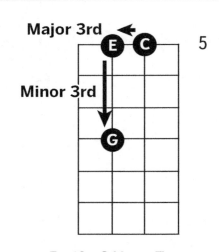

Fig.16 - C Major Triad

MAJOR CHORDS

Chords are built from triads. Take the notes from a triad—played together, they make a chord. Optionally, rearrange them or combine them with the same notes in another octave and you'll have another way to play the chord.

In the universe of music, there are many scales. Some are major, some are minor...

Major scales give us major triads. Major triads give us major chords.

G MAJOR SCALE, TRIAD AND CHORD

Here's the G Major scale. Notice how the half-steps are again in-between the 3rd and 4th, and 7th and 8th notes. The # symbol indicates the note is "F sharp", one half-step higher than F.

Fig.17 - G Major Scale Note Names

And here is how to find the G Major scale on the fretboard. It should look familiar. Notice how it's the same shape as the C Major scale.

Play the G Major scale in Figures 18 and 19.

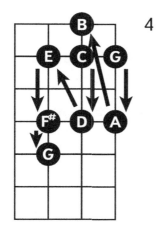

Fig.18 - G Major Scale
Starting on 4th String

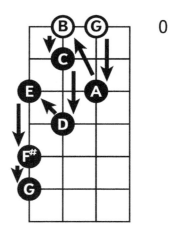

Fig.19 - G Major Scale
Starting on 3rd String

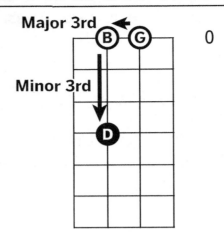

Here's the triad, containing the 1st, 3rd and 5th degrees of the G Major scale.

The only thing separating this triad from a chord is that all three notes can't be played individually here. When banjoists make a chord from a triad, they arrange these notes on different strings to make them playable simultaneously. The G would be on one string, B on another and D on yet another.

FIG.20 - G MAJOR TRIAD

Additionally, banjoists, guitarists and keyboardists often double some of these notes with their octave counterparts to create a much fuller sound.

Visualizing Triads

When learning triads, pay special attention to the root note. Always visualize the triad as it's built on the root.

SEEING MUSIC

Did you notice how the G Major scale uses the same shape as the C Major scale you learned earlier?

The G Major scale uses the same shape as C Major, but starts on a different note, G. The scale is changed to G Major.

Putting It Together

Major scales are made of whole and half-steps.

Major triads contain the 1st, 3rd and 5th degrees of the major scale.

Major chords are made from their corresponding scale's major triad.

Pay special attention to the root and visualize the chord as built on the root.

HOW TO USE THIS BOOK

READ THIS FIRST

Just as the universe is a big, big place, any scale can be used in a million ways. This book will help you explore many of them. Each chapter gives you the high points of each scale: how it is spelled, related chords and some common uses. The exercises can be performed in many different ways, thus making numerous possibilities and providing a challenge to every level of banjo player.

The examples of chords and scale substitutions here are only mere examples and by no means complete. There are simply too many chords and scales in the musical universe to be listed this book. Use the examples as suggestions to guide you when making harmonic choices for a given scale.

Each scale has a unique combination of intervals. No two scales are alike. It's this combination of intervals that define the scale, so they are stated here. An example of each scale with the root note C is spelled.

A capital "M" denotes a major interval, lower case "m" denotes a minor interval and "P" indicates a perfect interval. The symbol "M3" would represent a Major 3rd.

SPELLING

Half-Steps

Intervals	R	M2	M3	P4	P5	M6	M7	R
Example	C	D	E	F	G	A	B	C

COMMON STYLE AND GENRE USE

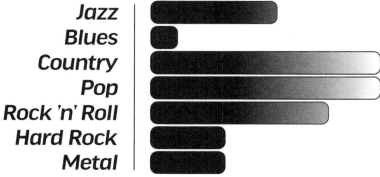

Jazz
Blues
Country
Pop
Rock 'n' Roll
Hard Rock
Metal

This section lists some popular genres and a prevalence of the use of the scale in that style. No matter what your genre or style, all scales are worth studying. And of course, there are no rules that a scale can't be used in a given style or genre. The content of this section is should be seen as highly subjective and as a musician, you're free to experiment!

CHORD FAMILY

Maj7   Maj9   13   6/9

All chords come from their related scales. As such, these related scales sound terrific when used over those chords. Listed in this section are a few of the more common chords that will sound great with the chapter scale.

If you're not familiar with an indicated chord type, have a look at the last chapter, *Chord and Mode Reference*.

SCALE SUBSTITUTIONS

Any time a given scale can be used, there are usually several alternative scales that can be substituted in its place. These *substitutions* provide an improvising musician with options for how to play a given passage. Variety can be exciting and substituting an appropriate scale can help keep the listener interested.

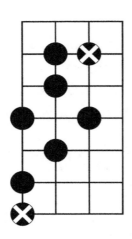
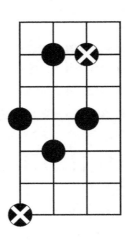

Sometimes the substituted scale is a subset of the original, as is the case with the Major Pentatonic and Ionian. Other times, the substitution carries several significant notes from the original and also some new, more colorful notes which are not found in the original scale. Such an example is Locrian and Ionian. These type of substitutions may not be appropriate for a given song or style, or they may clash with the melody or other parts of the arrangement, so good musical discretion is needed.

SCALES

Any scale can be played in several ways and found in several places on the fretboard. Each scale is presented here in a one-octave form, either starting on the 4th string or the 3rd string. These versions don't use open strings and as such, can easily be moved up and down the fretboard to transpose the key.

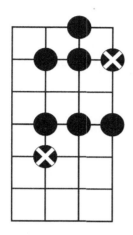

FIG.21 - SCALE STARTING ON 4TH STRING

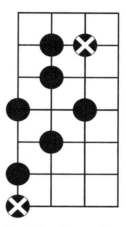

FIG.22 - SCALE STARTING ON 3RD STRING

You'll notice that these scales don't specify any key or root. The key of the scale is entirely up to you. The fretboard dot with the "X" through it indicates the root of the scale. To play the scale in a given key, simply start the scale pattern on this note.

Also, each scale is displayed in various forms which are convenient to different fingerings. For maximum musicianship, it's best to be able to start a scale with either the first finger, pinky finger or one of the middle fingers. These various layouts give banjo players options for playability and tone choice. Try each layout of the scale and notice the subtle differences in tone as the notes are arranged in different locations on the fretboard.

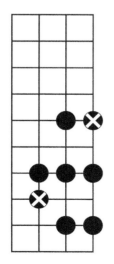

FIG.23 - SCALE STARTING WITH 1ST FINGER

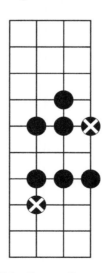

FIG.24 - SCALE STARTING WITH 2ND FINGER

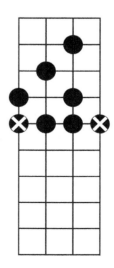

FIG.25 - SCALE STARTING WITH 4TH FINGER

EXERCISES

Are you starting to feel overwhelmed by the many options you have for mastering these scales? That's understandable! All of the musical universe is built from scales and there are never-ending combinations of them. Take a deep breath and just start simply, learning each scale in it's simplest form as you go. Whatever form seems simplest to you is a fine place to start.

If you're up for greater challenges, these scale exercises will keep you expanding your horizons for quite a while. A great technique when creating melodies is to play notes from a scale, either in linear fashion or in a triadic manner - progressing by 3rds. These little bits of melody may ascend or descend along the scale. As such, it's beneficial to practice scales in this way - little bits of scales ascending or descending linearly or triadically.

> *Remember that the purpose of these exercises is to increase your musicianship. Don't worry about speed until you're connecting the notes smoothly and musically. The result should be a very controlled and pleasing musical experience. Audiences prefer a nice, slow and controlled piece of music over a speedy but sloppy mess.*

Further, you can practice these bits of melody in various ways. Examine this diagram:

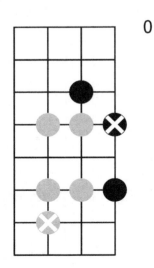

0

The entire scale is represented and the black dots indicate the fragment to be played. Three notes are indicated: C, D and E. But, the *order* of the notes is *not* indicated. That means it is up to you!

One way to play this fragment is C, D, E   Another way is in reverse order: E, D, C

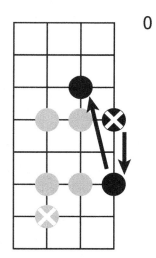

0

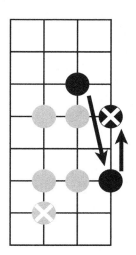

0

Here is an example of how to play the same exercise in two different ways. The arrows indicate the order of the notes.

UPWARD FRAGMENTS

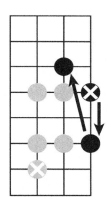

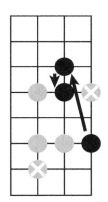

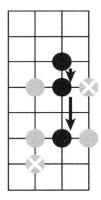

etc..

FIG.26 - ASCENDING SCALE EXERCISE - UPWARD FRAGMENTS

DOWNWARD FRAGMENTS

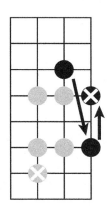

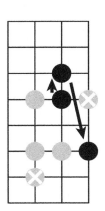

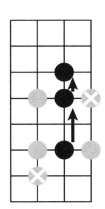

etc..

FIG.27 - ASCENDING SCALE EXERCISE - DOWNWARD FRAGMENTS

Likewise, triadic lines can be played in reverse order.

UPWARD MOTION

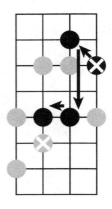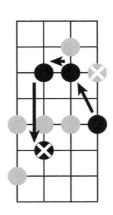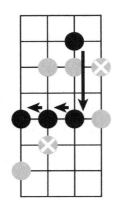

FIG.28 - ASCENDING 3RDS EXERCISE - UPWARD MOTION

etc..

DOWNWARD MOTION

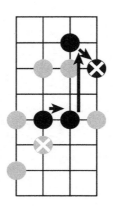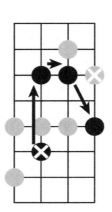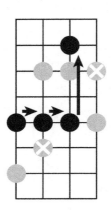

FIG.29 - ASCENDING 3RDS EXERCISE - DOWNWARD MOTION

etc..

Are you hungry for even more challenges? How about trying linear groups of four notes, instead of just three? Groups of 5? Or play the three note group both ascending and descending: C, D, E, D, C; D, E, F, E, D; E, F, G, F, E, etc.

Try any of the exercises with a steady crescendo or decrescendo. For example, play the first note of the exercise as softly as possible, growing a little louder with each note. By the time you get to the last note, be at maximum volume. Then try the reverse, starting loudly and growing softer to the end.

How about rhythm? Try any of these exercises and give the notes a little swing.

Are you starting to see the infinite possibilities for playing these scales? Recombining small fragments of the scale in new arrangements and including variations in dynamics and rhythm is both great for your musicianship and it makes a fun challenge that keeps things interesting.

24 LEFT-HANDED BANJO SCALES INFINITY: A SEEING MUSIC METHOD BOOK

MODES AND MODAL THEORY

IN THIS UNIVERSE

The modes of a major scale are directly related to that scale. You'll learn how to create all 7 modes and be able to apply them to melodies.

WHAT ARE MODES?

Modes are scales built from the notes of a major scale. They're different versions which all contain the same notes, starting on a different note.

Here are the 7 modes of C Major.

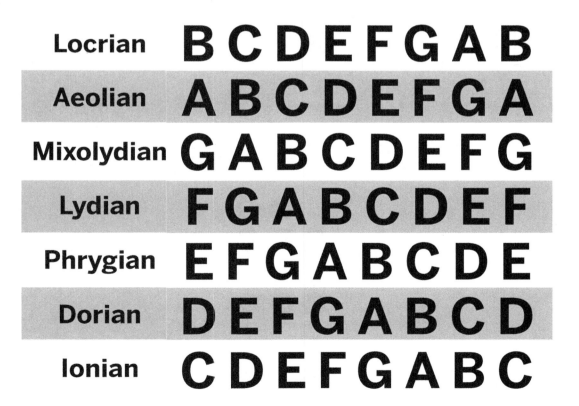

FIG.30 - MODES OF C MAJOR

Modes on the Fretboard

When played on the 2nd, 3rd and 4th strings, the modes look like this:

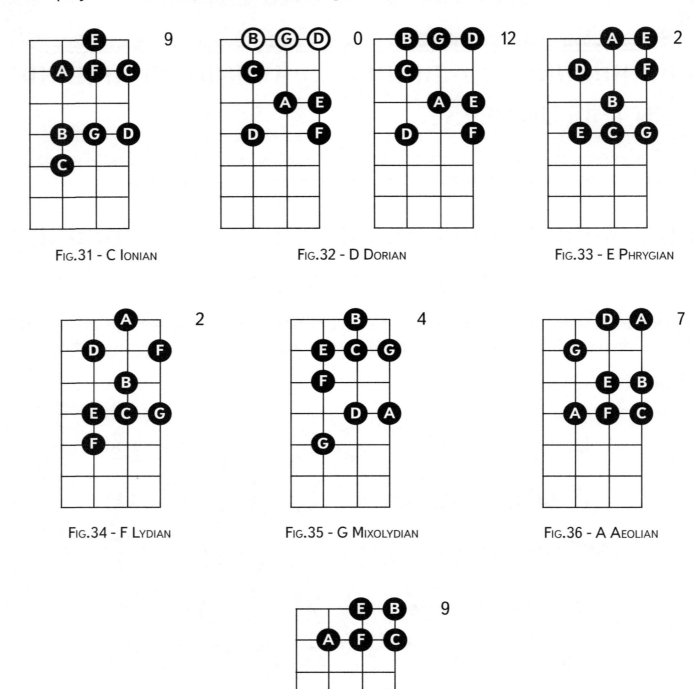

FIG.31 - C IONIAN

FIG.32 - D DORIAN

FIG.33 - E PHRYGIAN

FIG.34 - F LYDIAN

FIG.35 - G MIXOLYDIAN

FIG.36 - A AEOLIAN

FIG.37 - B LOCRIAN

Notice how C Major itself, is considered a mode, Ionian. If you're familiar with the natural minor scale, you can see it again here, called A Aeolian.

Now take another look at the scales, noting the similarities between many of them. Ionian, Lydian and Mixolydian all contain their own root, major 3rd and perfect 5th. For this reason, they all sound a bit similar, like the major scales from earlier. Give them a play, and notice the sort of "family resemblence".

Having a minor flavor, Dorian, Phyrgian and Aeolian have their own root, minor 3rd and perfect 5th. Play these now and note their similarities.

Because of their similarities, sophisticated musicians will often substitute these modes for the more traditional minor or major scales. They share enough with the more common scales to be appropriate, yet ofter a little spice when variety is sought.

Of course, every major key has similar associated modes built upon the unique scale tones of that original scale.

HOW ARE MODES USED?

One manner in which modes are used, such as in jazz, progressive or punk rock, jam or psychedelic rock, is to use them as "blankets" to create colorful and unexpected melody and harmony. Soloists will choose a particular mode for solos and create melodies from it. Rarely changing the tonal center, these scales are thrown over a large chunk of the progression like a blanket.

Another way modes are used is to build melodies or chords in ways that blend well with the chord progression. Melodies built using a modal approach flow well from one chord to another because the modes share so many notes.

Try some modes as a blanket over these progressions. Instead of improvising over the indicated D sharp9, try swapping either D Minor Pentatonic or D Mixolydian over this progression.

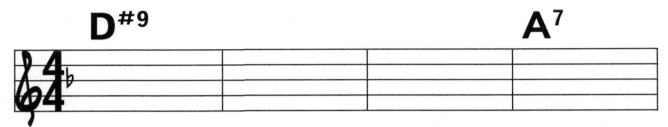

FIG.38 - D #9 PROGRESSION

For accompaniment reference

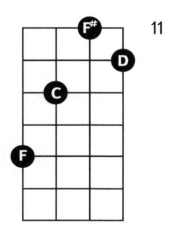

FIG.39 - D #9 CHORD

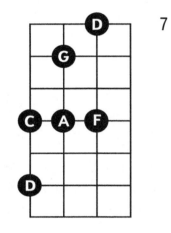

FIG.41 - D MINOR PENTATONIC

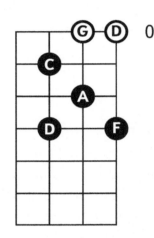

FIG.42 - D MINOR PENTATONIC

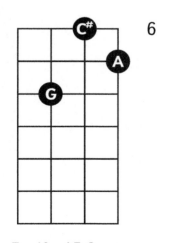

FIG.40 - A7 CHORD

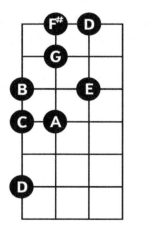

FIG.43 - D MIXOLYDIAN

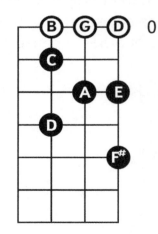

FIG.44 - D MIXOLYDIAN

Ready for a bigger challenge? Revisit Figure 38 using D Mixolydian and A Mixolydian over the D #9 and A7 chords, respectively.

PUTTING IT TOGETHER

There are seven modes of the major scale.

Each mode is unique in its combination of degrees, making it well suited in "blanket" applications.

Ionian, Lydian and Mixolydian have major-sounding traits.

Dorian, Phrygian and Aeolian have minor-sounding traits.

Modes can be used to create melodies that flow well from chord to chord in a progression.

IONIAN

IN THIS UNIVERSE

Ionian is also known as Major. Containing the Major 3rd, 7th, 2nd and 6th, it is suited well for Major 7, Major 9 and Major 13th chords.

OVERVIEW

Spelling

Intervals	R	M2	M3	P4	P5	M6	M7	R
Example	C	D	E	F	G	A	B	C

FIG.45 - IONIAN SPELLING

Common Style and Genre Use

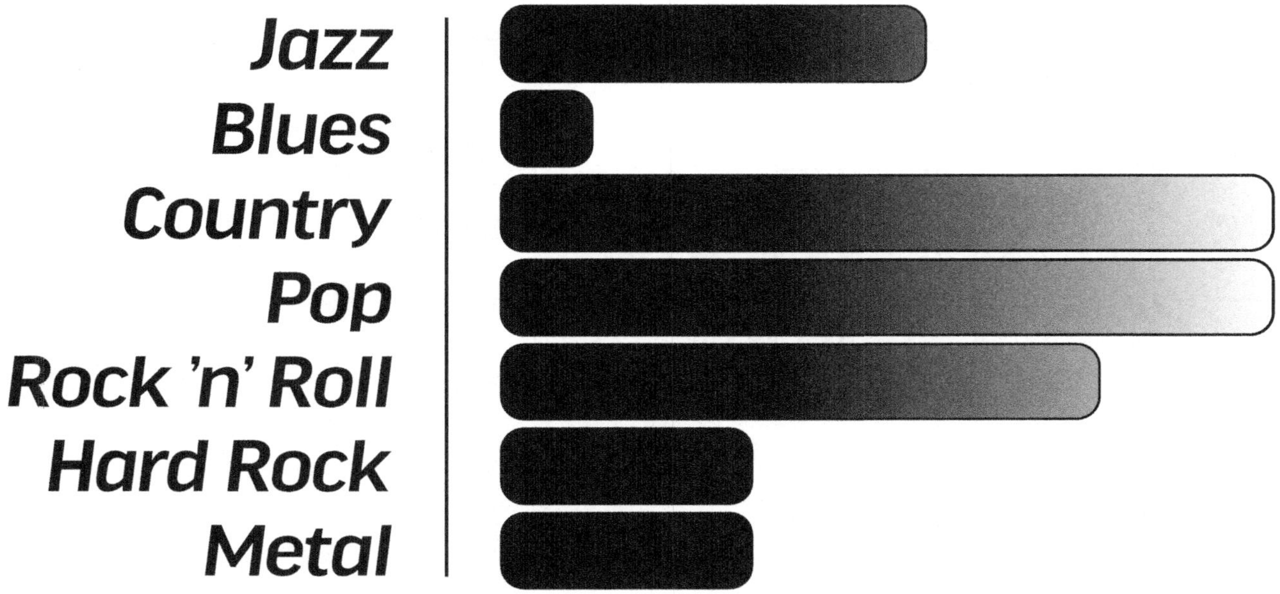

Jazz
Blues
Country
Pop
Rock 'n' Roll
Hard Rock
Metal

FIG.46 - IONIAN COMMON USAGE

Chord Family

Containing a Major 2nd, 3rd, 6th and 7th makes Ionian a great candidate for use with extended Major chords.

Maj   Maj7   Maj9

13   6/9

Fig.47 - Ionian Chord Family

Scale Substitutions

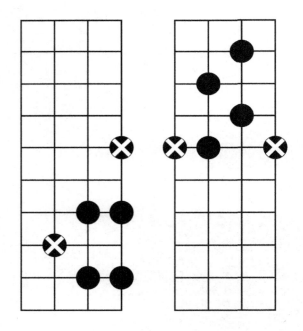

Fig.48 - Major Pentatonic Scale

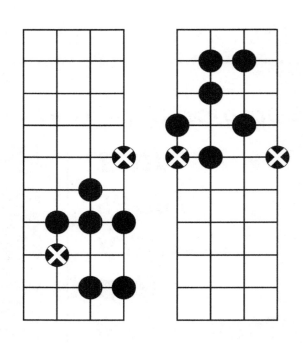

Fig.49 - Lydian Scale

SCALES

STARTING ON 4TH STRING

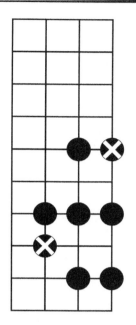
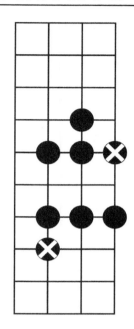
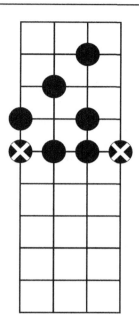

FIG.50 - IONIAN BEGINNING ON 4TH STRING

STARTING ON 3RD STRING

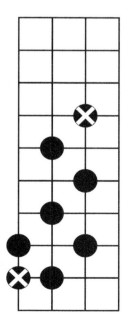
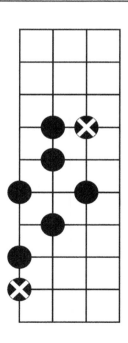
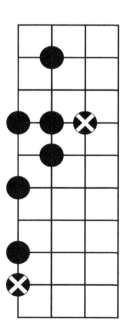

FIG.51 - IONIAN BEGINNING ON 3RD STRING

IONIAN 33

LINEAR 4TH STRING

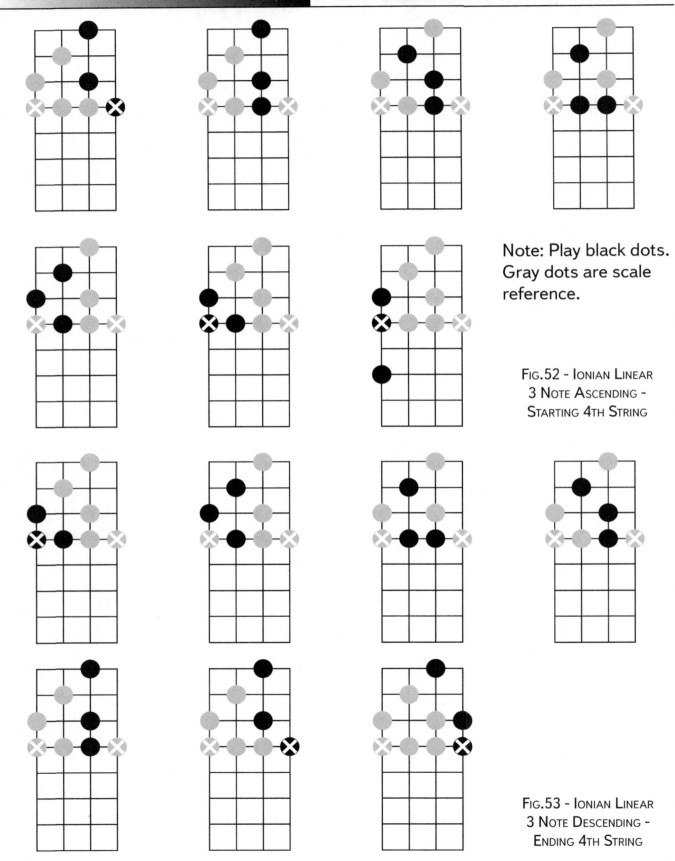

Note: Play black dots. Gray dots are scale reference.

Fig.52 - Ionian Linear 3 Note Ascending - Starting 4th String

Fig.53 - Ionian Linear 3 Note Descending - Ending 4th String

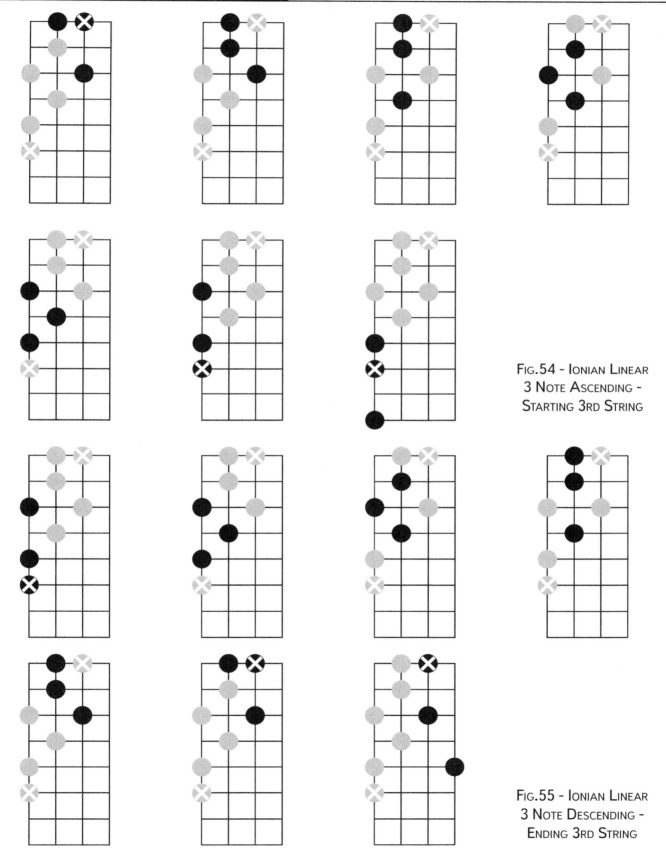

FIG.54 - IONIAN LINEAR
3 NOTE ASCENDING -
STARTING 3RD STRING

FIG.55 - IONIAN LINEAR
3 NOTE DESCENDING -
ENDING 3RD STRING

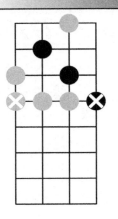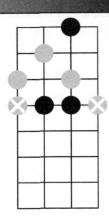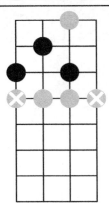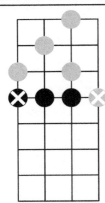

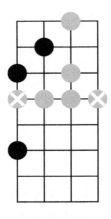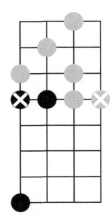

FIG.56 - IONIAN
3RDS ASCENDING -
STARTING 4TH STRING

3RDS DESCENDING

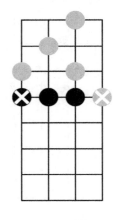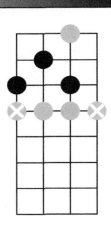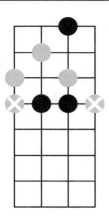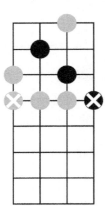

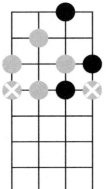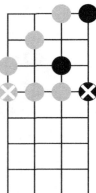

FIG.57 - IONIAN
3RDS DESCENDING -
ENDING 3RD STRING

DORIAN

||||||||||||||||||||||||||||||||||||||||||||||||||||||||||||||||||||||||||||||

IN THIS UNIVERSE

Dorian is a minor flavor. Containing the minor 3rd and 7th but also the major 2nd and 6th, it is suited well for many major and minor chords.

||||||||||||||||||||||||||||||||||||||||||||||||||||||||||||||||||||||||||||||

OVERVIEW

Spelling

Intervals	R	M2	m3	P4	P5	M6	m7	R
Example	C	D	E♭	F	G	A	B♭	C

FIG.58 - DORIAN SPELLING

Common Style and Genre Use

Jazz
Blues
Country
Pop
Rock 'n' Roll
Hard Rock
Metal

FIG.59 - DORIAN COMMON USAGE

Chord Family

Containing the minor 3rd and 7th, but also the major 6th, Dorian has a principally minor flavor, but may also work well with major chords.

min   min7   min9

FIG.60 - DORIAN CHORD FAMILY

Scale Substitutions

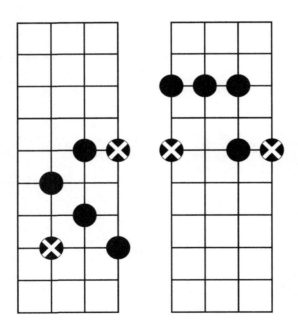

FIG.61 - MINOR PENTATONIC SCALE

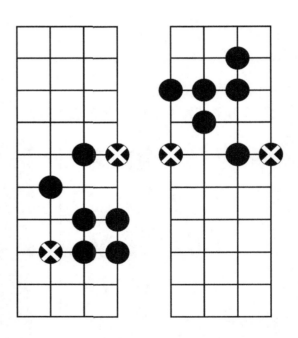

FIG.62 - AEOLIAN SCALE

SCALES

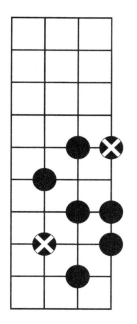
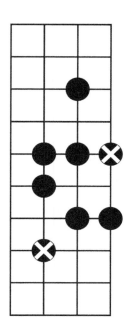
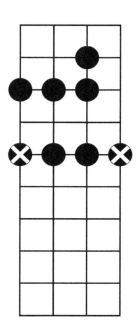

FIG.63 - DORIAN BEGINNING ON 4TH STRING

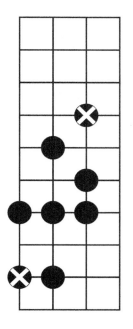
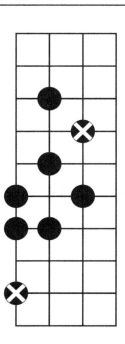
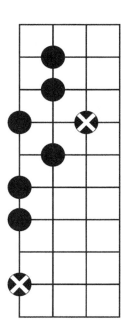

FIG.64 - DORIAN BEGINNING ON 3RD STRING

LINEAR 4TH STRING

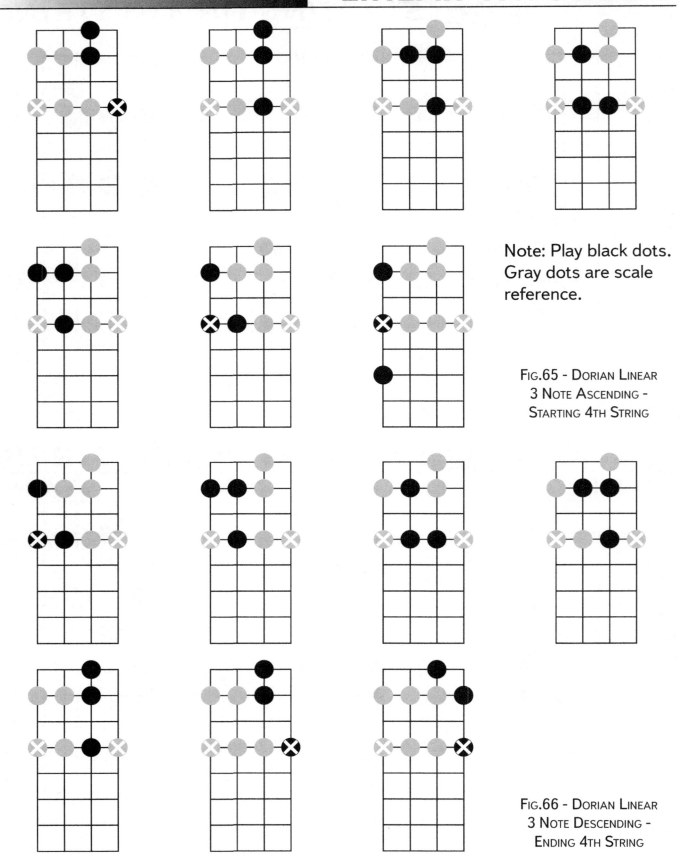

Note: Play black dots. Gray dots are scale reference.

FIG.65 - DORIAN LINEAR
3 NOTE ASCENDING -
STARTING 4TH STRING

FIG.66 - DORIAN LINEAR
3 NOTE DESCENDING -
ENDING 4TH STRING

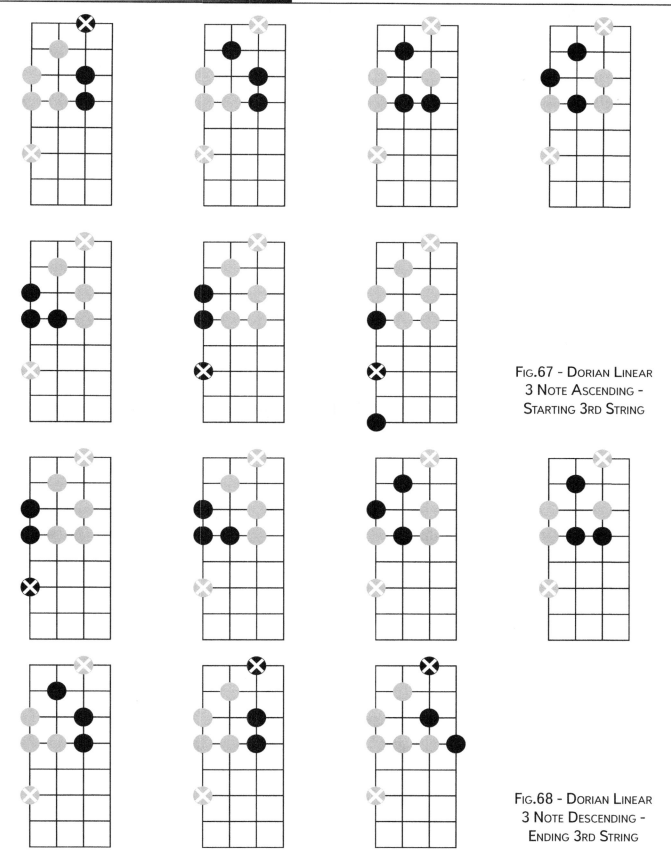

Fig.67 - Dorian Linear
3 Note Ascending -
Starting 3rd String

Fig.68 - Dorian Linear
3 Note Descending -
Ending 3rd String

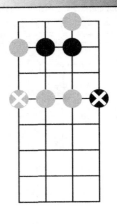
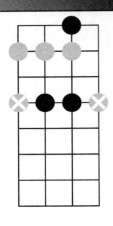
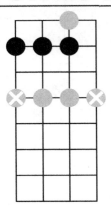
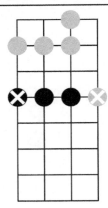

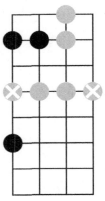
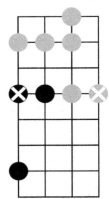
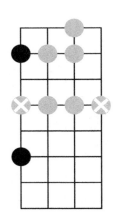

FIG.69 - DORIAN
3RDS ASCENDING -
STARTING 4TH STRING

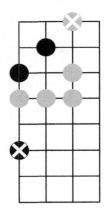
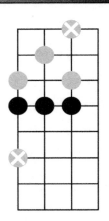
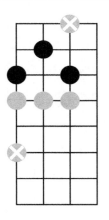
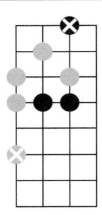

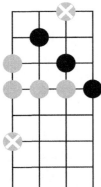
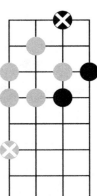
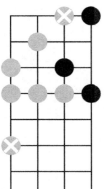

FIG.70 - DORIAN
3RDS DESCENDING -
ENDING 3RD STRING

PHRYGIAN

||||||||||||||||||||||||||||||||||||||||||||||||||||||||||||||||||||

IN THIS UNIVERSE

Phrygian has an exotic minor flavor. Containing the minor 2nd, 3rd, 6th and 7th, it's a favorite among jazz musicians and metal guitarists, as well.

||||||||||||||||||||||||||||||||||||||||||||||||||||||||||||||||||||

OVERVIEW

Spelling

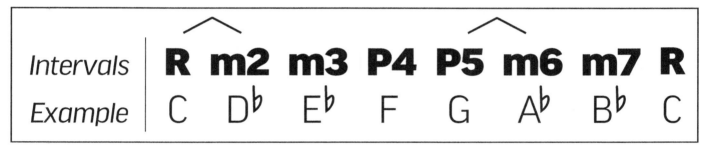

Intervals	R	m2	m3	P4	P5	m6	m7	R
Example	C	D♭	E♭	F	G	A♭	B♭	C

FIG.71 - PHRYGIAN SPELLING

Common Style and Genre Use

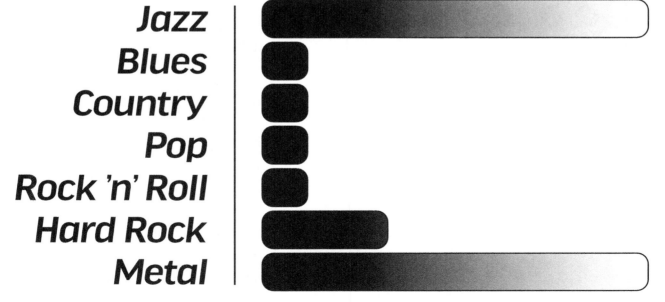

Jazz
Blues
Country
Pop
Rock 'n' Roll
Hard Rock
Metal

FIG.72 - PHRYGIAN COMMON USAGE

Chord Family

Containing the minor 2nd, 3rd and 7th, Phrygian has an exotic minor flavor all its own.

min7♭9   ♭9

Fig.73 - Phrygian Chord Family

Scale Substitutions

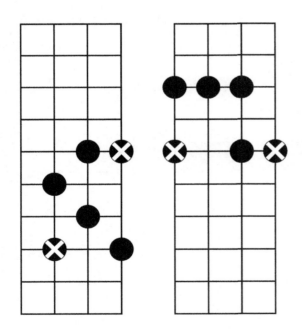

Fig.74 - Minor Pentatonic Scale

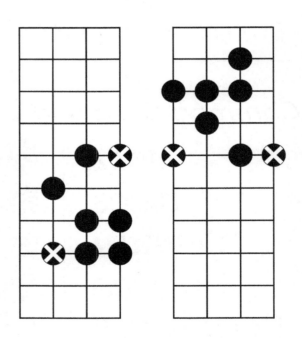

Fig.75 - Aeolian Scale

SCALES

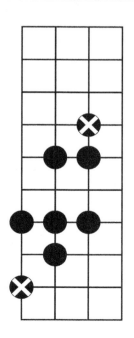
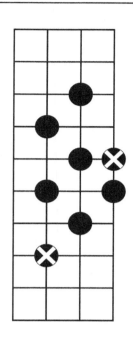
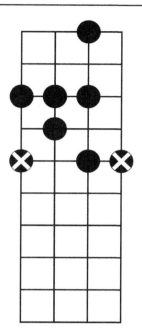

Fig.76 - Phrygian Beginning on 4th String

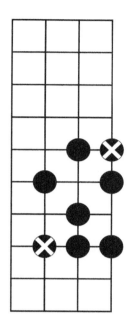
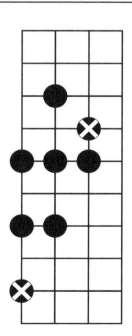
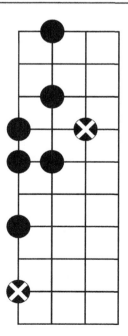

Fig.77 - Phrygian Beginning on 3rd String

LINEAR 4TH STRING

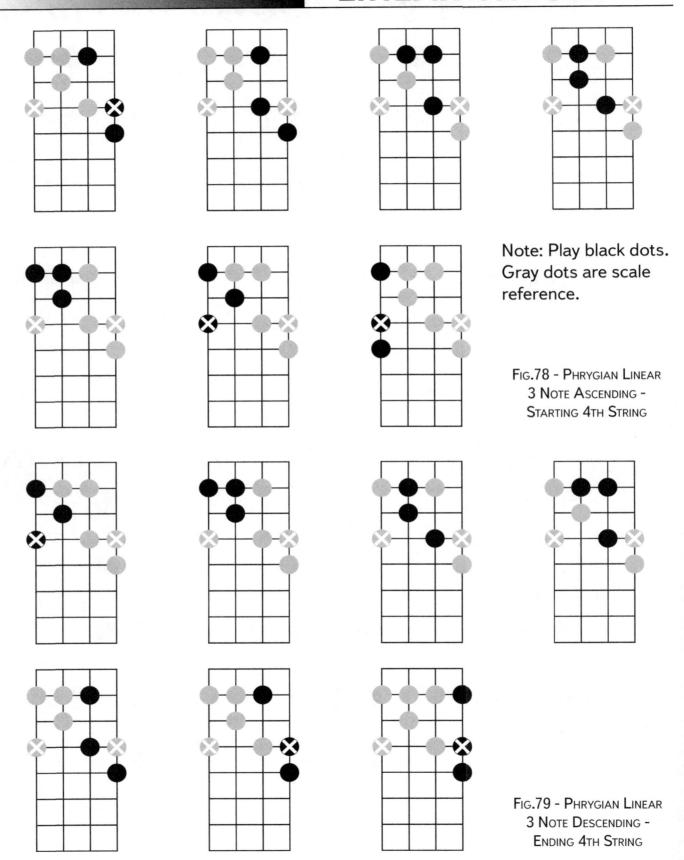

Note: Play black dots. Gray dots are scale reference.

FIG.78 - PHRYGIAN LINEAR 3 NOTE ASCENDING - STARTING 4TH STRING

FIG.79 - PHRYGIAN LINEAR 3 NOTE DESCENDING - ENDING 4TH STRING

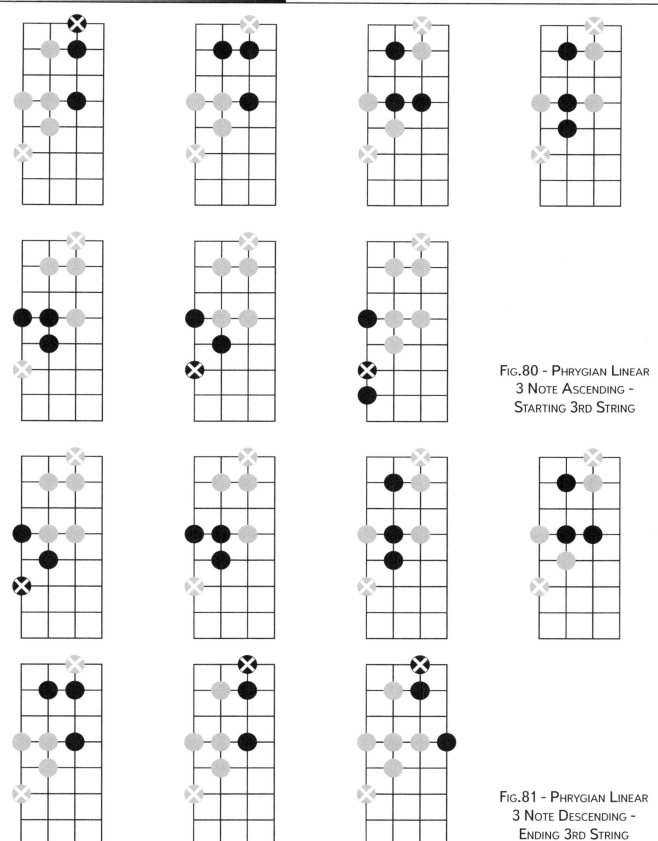

FIG.80 - PHRYGIAN LINEAR
3 NOTE ASCENDING -
STARTING 3RD STRING

FIG.81 - PHRYGIAN LINEAR
3 NOTE DESCENDING -
ENDING 3RD STRING

PHRYGIAN 47

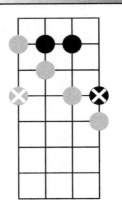
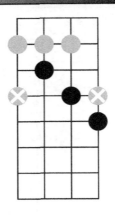
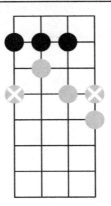
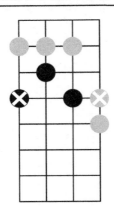

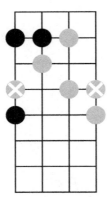
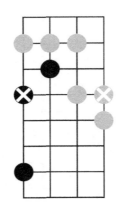
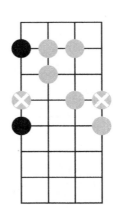

FIG.82 - PHRYGIAN
3RDS ASCENDING -
STARTING 4TH STRING

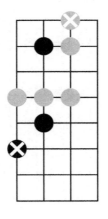
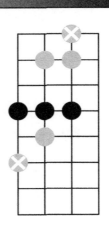
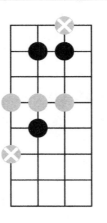
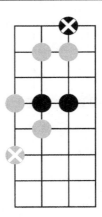

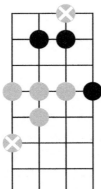
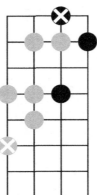
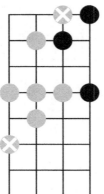

FIG.83 - PHRYGIAN
3RDS DESCENDING -
ENDING 3RD STRING

LYDIAN

||||||||||||||||||||||||||||||||||||||||||||||||||||||||||||||||||||||

IN THIS UNIVERSE

Having a major sound, Lydian is a close relative to Ionian. The two differ by just one note, the 4th degree, which is raised in Lydian.

||||||||||||||||||||||||||||||||||||||||||||||||||||||||||||||||||||||

OVERVIEW

Spelling

Intervals	R	M2	M3	#4	P5	M6	M7	R
Example	C	D	E	F#	G	A	B	C

FIG.84 - LYDIAN SPELLING

Common Style and Genre Use

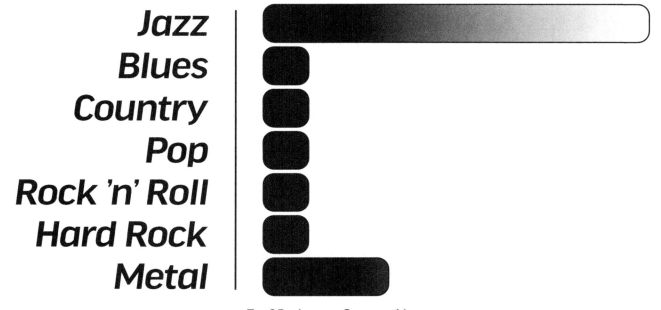

- Jazz
- Blues
- Country
- Pop
- Rock 'n' Roll
- Hard Rock
- Metal

FIG.85 - LYDIAN COMMON USAGE

Chord Family

Closely resembling Ionian (major), Lydian is perfectly suited for many extended major chords.

Maj   Maj7   Maj9

13   6/9   Maj7#11

FIG.86 - LYDIAN CHORD FAMILY

Scale Substitutions

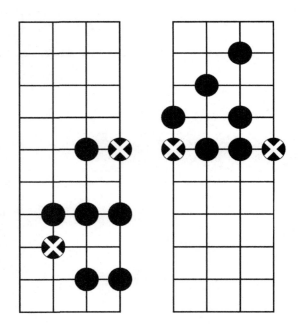

FIG.87 - IONIAN SCALE

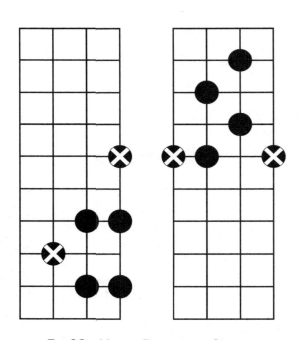

FIG.88 - MAJOR PENTATONIC SCALE

SCALES

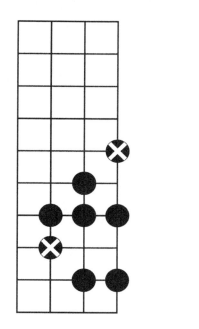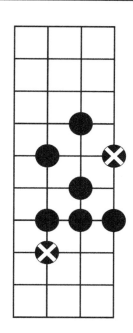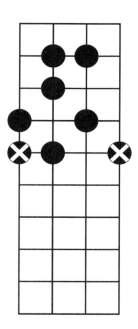

FIG.89 - LYDIAN BEGINNING ON 4TH STRING

STARTING ON 3RD STRING

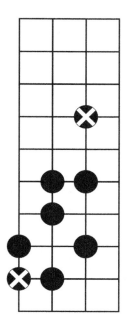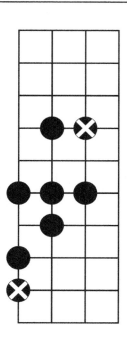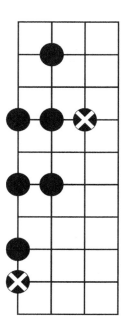

FIG.90 - LYDIAN BEGINNING ON 3RD STRING

LINEAR 4TH STRING

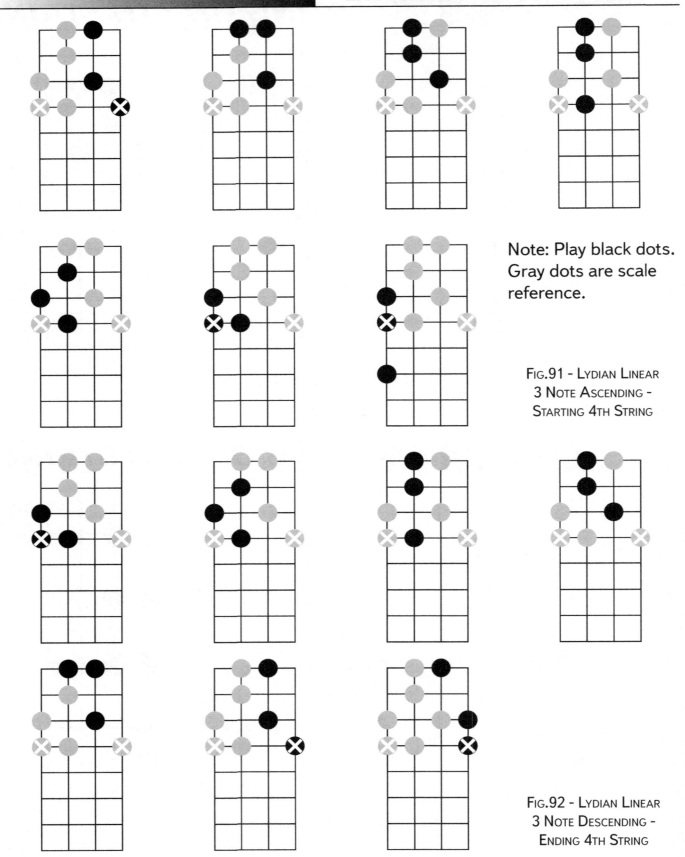

Note: Play black dots. Gray dots are scale reference.

FIG.91 - LYDIAN LINEAR 3 NOTE ASCENDING - STARTING 4TH STRING

FIG.92 - LYDIAN LINEAR 3 NOTE DESCENDING - ENDING 4TH STRING

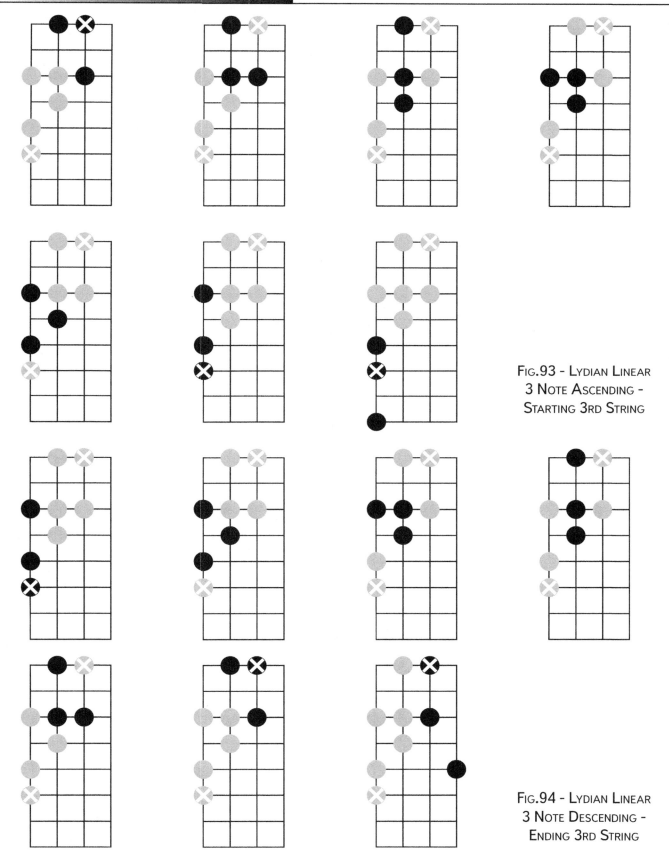

FIG.93 - LYDIAN LINEAR
3 NOTE ASCENDING -
STARTING 3RD STRING

FIG.94 - LYDIAN LINEAR
3 NOTE DESCENDING -
ENDING 3RD STRING

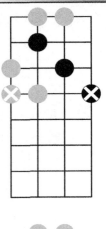
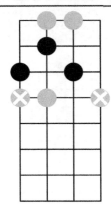
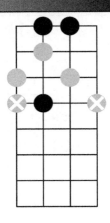
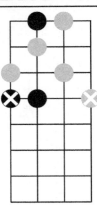

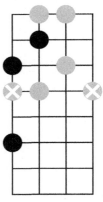
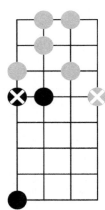
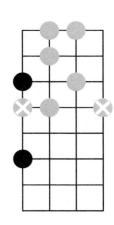

FIG.95 - LYDIAN
3RDS ASCENDING -
STARTING 4TH STRING

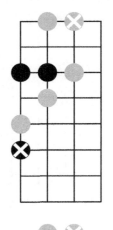
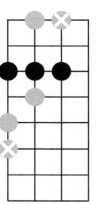
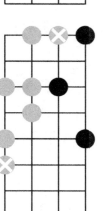
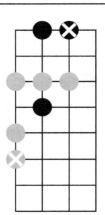

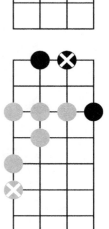

FIG.96 - LYDIAN
3RDS DESCENDING -
ENDING 3RD STRING

MIXOLYDIAN

IN THIS UNIVERSE

Mixolydian is the backbone of Blues and Jazz music, and is frequently heard in Classical music, as well.

OVERVIEW

Spelling

Intervals	R	M2	M3	P4	P5	M6	m7	R
Example	C	D	E	F	G	A	B♭	C

FIG.97 - MIXOLYDIAN SPELLING

Common Style and Genre Use

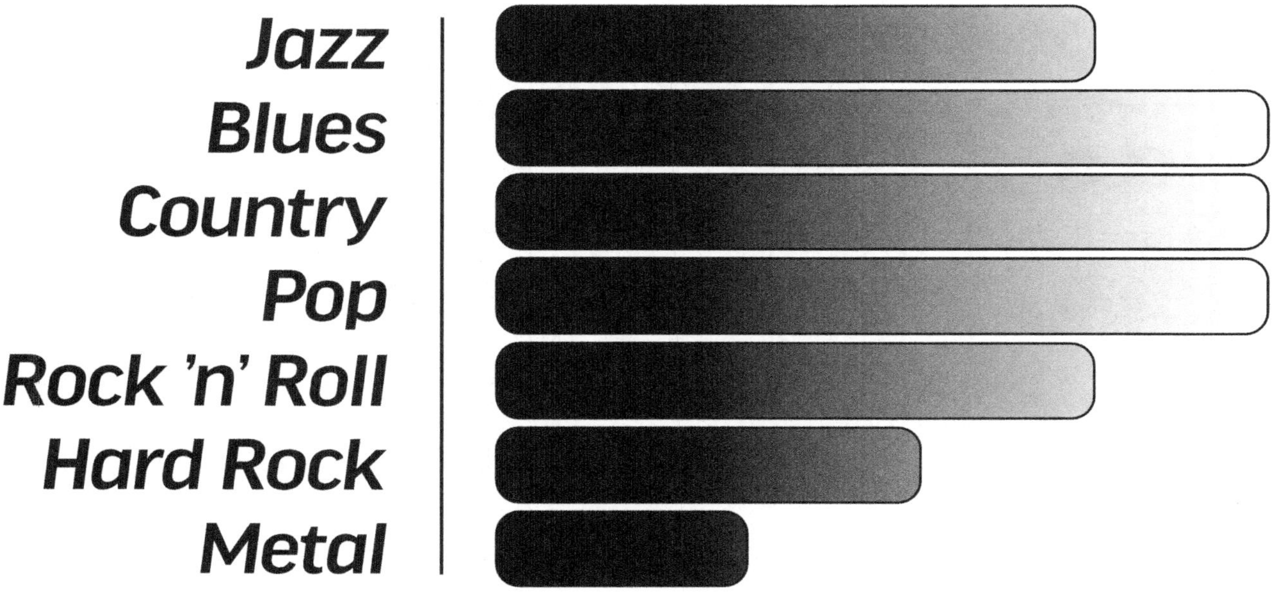

Jazz
Blues
Country
Pop
Rock 'n' Roll
Hard Rock
Metal

FIG.98 - MIXOLYDIAN COMMON USAGE

Chord Family

Containing the major 2nd, 3rd and minor 7th, Mixolydian sits perfectly among dominant 7th or 9th chords.

7   9   #9

Fig.99 - Mixolydian Chord Family

Scale Substitutions

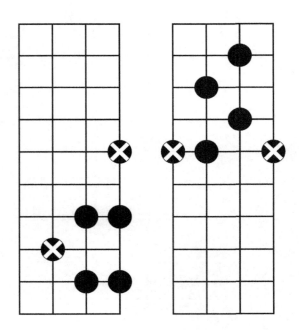

Fig.100 - Major Pentatonic Scale

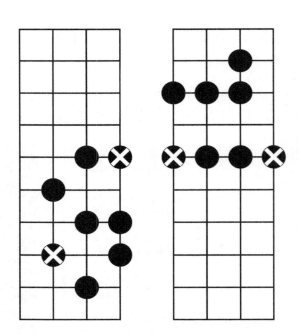

Fig.101 - Dorian Scale

SCALES

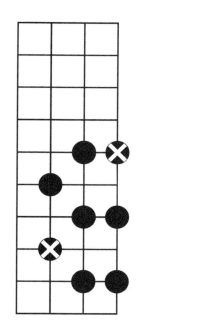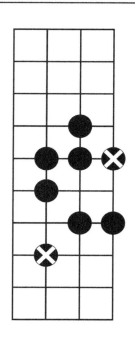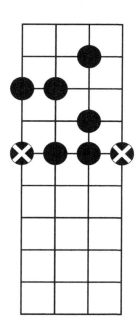

FIG.102 - MIXOLYDIAN BEGINNING ON 4TH STRING

STARTING ON 3RD STRING

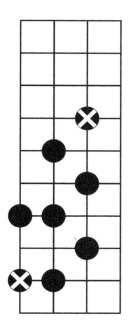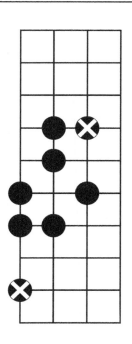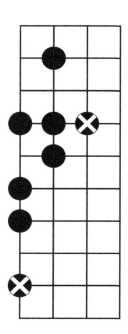

FIG.103 - MIXOLYDIAN BEGINNING ON 3RD STRING

LINEAR 4TH STRING

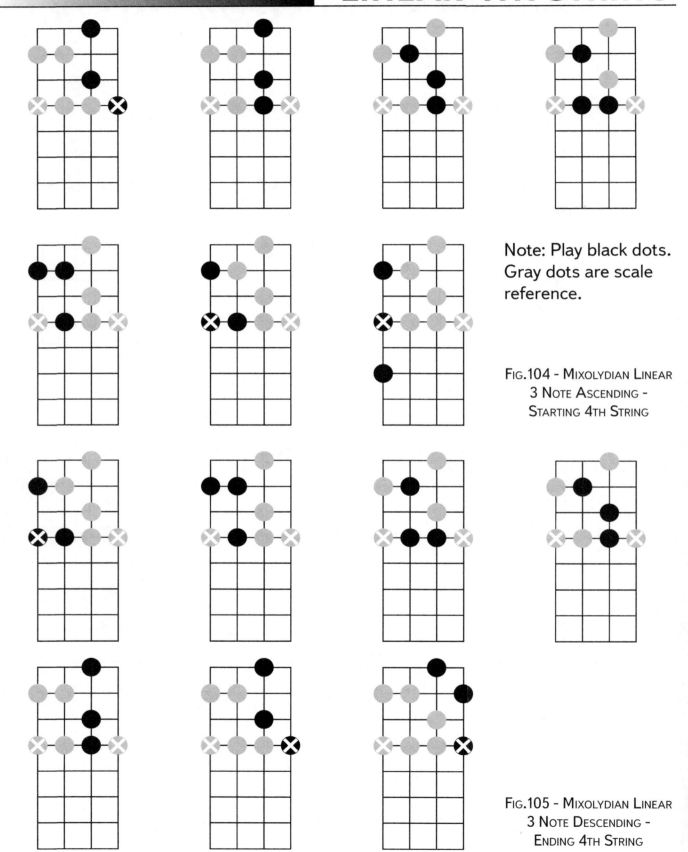

Note: Play black dots. Gray dots are scale reference.

FIG.104 - MIXOLYDIAN LINEAR 3 NOTE ASCENDING - STARTING 4TH STRING

FIG.105 - MIXOLYDIAN LINEAR 3 NOTE DESCENDING - ENDING 4TH STRING

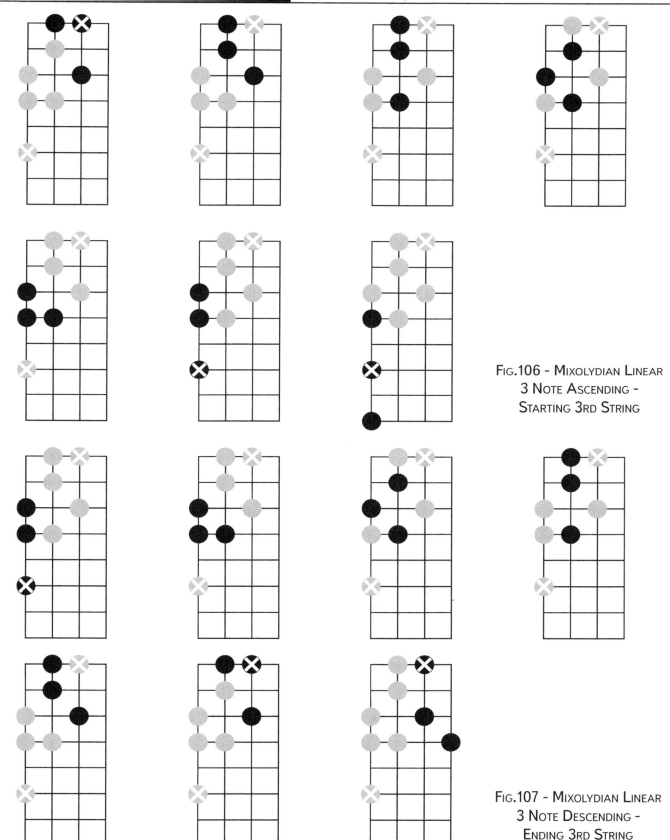

FIG.106 - MIXOLYDIAN LINEAR
3 NOTE ASCENDING -
STARTING 3RD STRING

FIG.107 - MIXOLYDIAN LINEAR
3 NOTE DESCENDING -
ENDING 3RD STRING

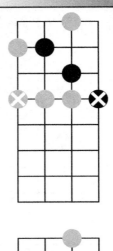 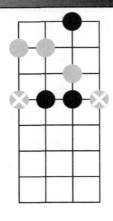 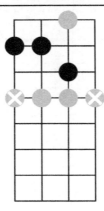 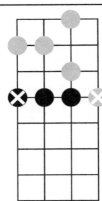

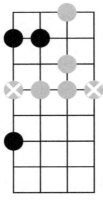 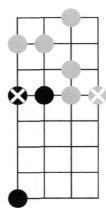 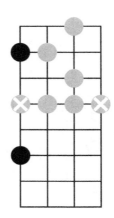

FIG.108 - MIXOLYDIAN
3RDS ASCENDING -
STARTING 4TH STRING

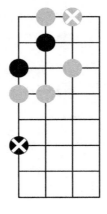 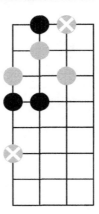 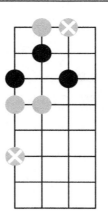 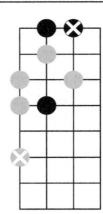

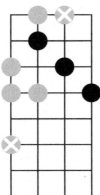 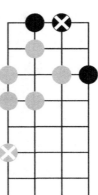 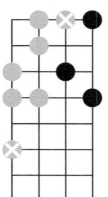

FIG.109 - MIXOLYDIAN
3RDS DESCENDING -
ENDING 3RD STRING

AEOLIAN

IN THIS UNIVERSE

Aeolian is also known as natural minor. Containing the minor 3rd and 7th it is one of the most widely used scales in all of music.

OVERVIEW

Spelling

Intervals	R	M2	m3	P4	P5	m6	m7	R
Example	C	D	E♭	F	G	A♭	B♭	C

FIG.110 - AEOLIAN SPELLING

Common Style and Genre Use

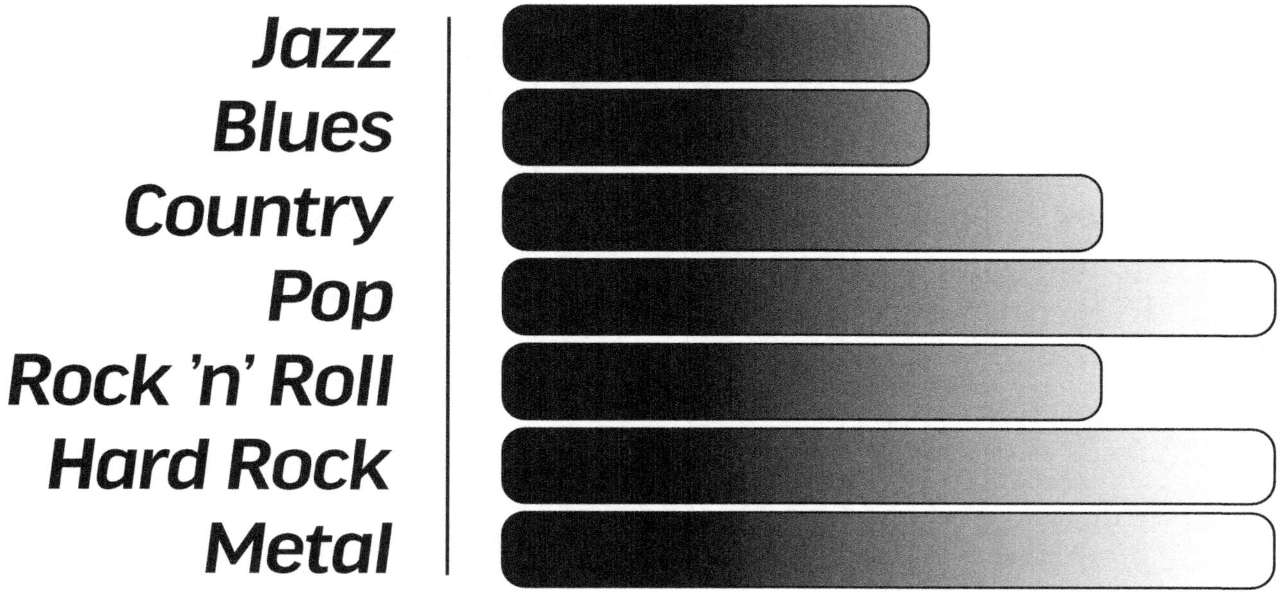

Jazz
Blues
Country
Pop
Rock 'n' Roll
Hard Rock
Metal

FIG.111 - AEOLIAN COMMON USAGE

Chord Family

Containing a Major 2nd, 3rd, 6th and 7th makes Ionian a great candidate for use with extended Major chords.

min   min7   min9

FIG.112 - AEOLIAN CHORD FAMILY

Scale Substitutions

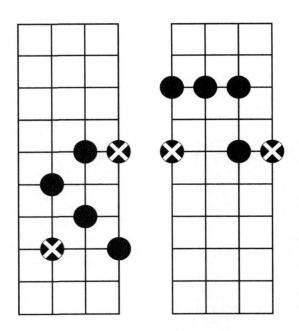

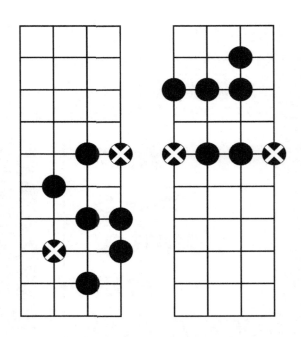

FIG.113 - MINOR PENTATONIC SCALE   FIG.114 - DORIAN SCALE

SCALES

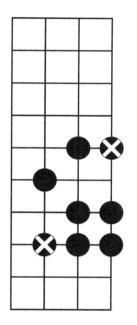
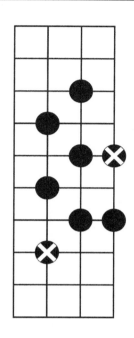
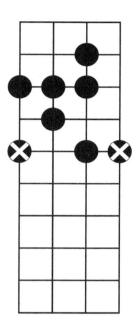

Fig.115 - Aeolian Beginning on 4th String

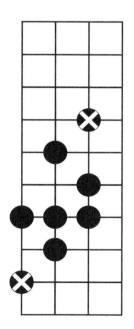
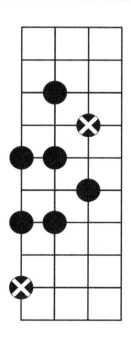
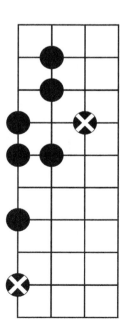

Fig.116 - Aeolian Beginning on 3rd String

LINEAR 4TH STRING

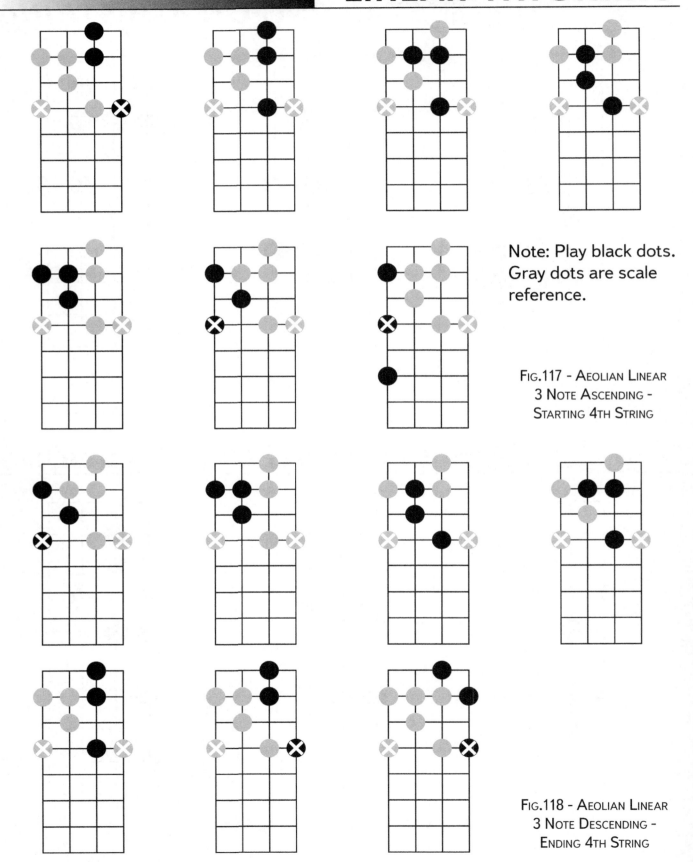

Note: Play black dots. Gray dots are scale reference.

Fig.117 - Aeolian Linear 3 Note Ascending - Starting 4th String

Fig.118 - Aeolian Linear 3 Note Descending - Ending 4th String

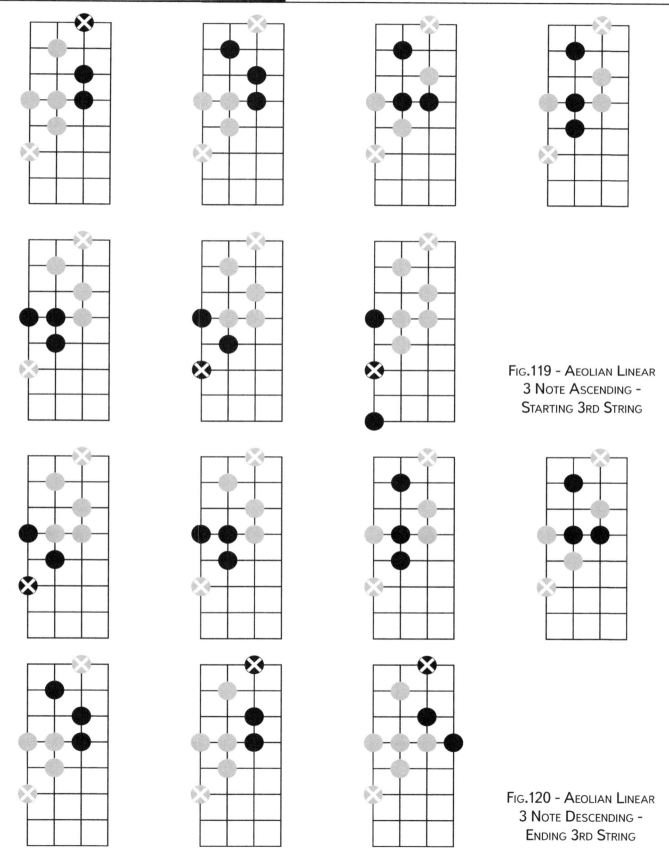

FIG.119 - AEOLIAN LINEAR
3 NOTE ASCENDING -
STARTING 3RD STRING

FIG.120 - AEOLIAN LINEAR
3 NOTE DESCENDING -
ENDING 3RD STRING

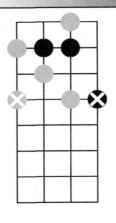
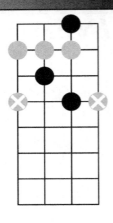
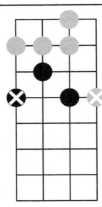
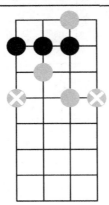

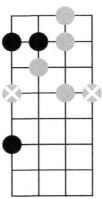
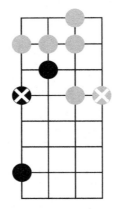
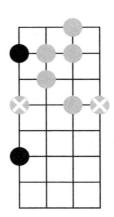

FIG.121 - AEOLIAN
3RDS ASCENDING -
STARTING 4TH STRING

3RDS DESCENDING

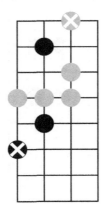
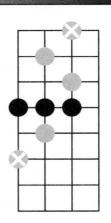
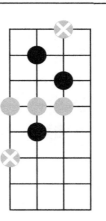
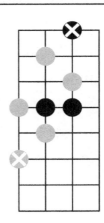

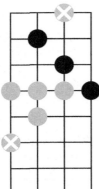
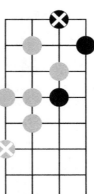
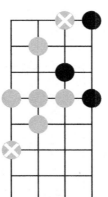

FIG.122 - AEOLIAN
3RDS DESCENDING -
ENDING 3RD STRING

LOCRIAN

IN THIS UNIVERSE

Locrian is a highly stylized minor sound. Containing the minor 2nd, 3rd, 6th, and 7th as well as the flatted 5th, it is full of flavor!

OVERVIEW

Spelling

Intervals	R m2 m3 P4 flat5 m6 m7 R
Example	C D♭ E♭ F G♭ A♭ B♭ C

Fig.123 - Locrian Spelling

Common Style and Genre Use

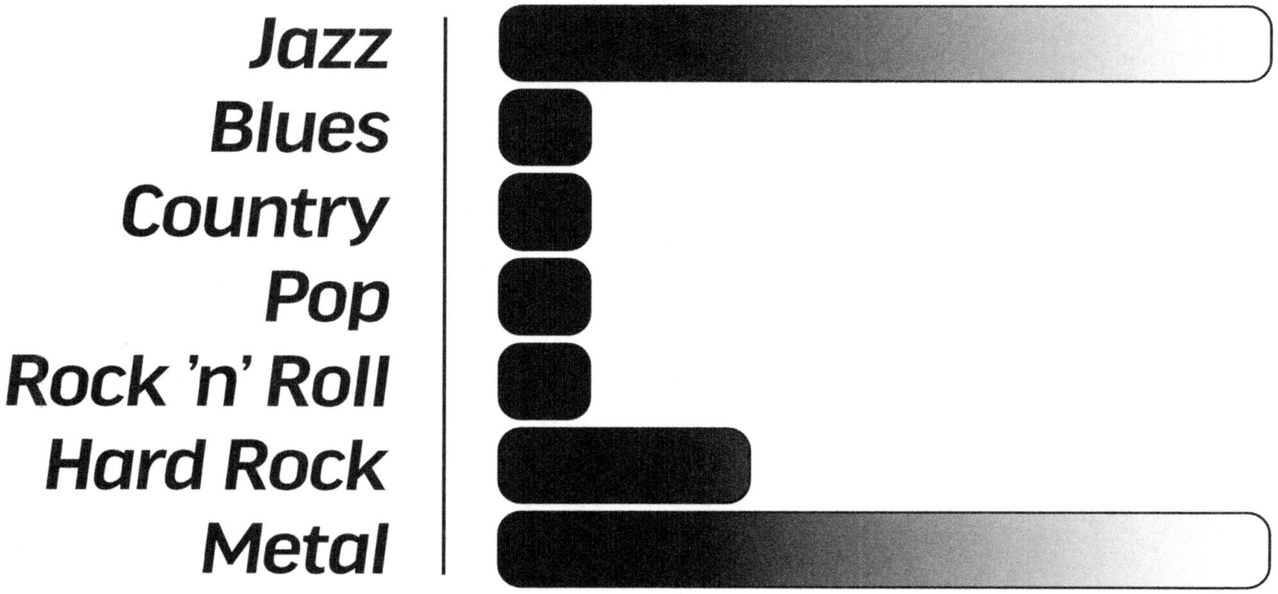

Jazz
Blues
Country
Pop
Rock 'n' Roll
Hard Rock
Metal

Fig.124 - Locrian Common Usage

Chord Family

Jazz and Metal players both enjoy the exotic and often strident sound of Locrian.

∅7   min7♭5   min7♭9

FIG.125 - LOCRIAN CHORD FAMILY

Scale Substitutions

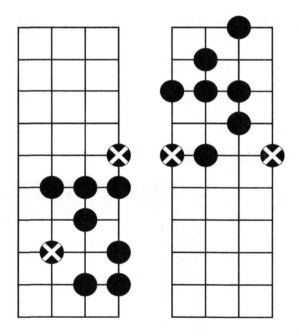

FIG.126 - HALF/WHOLE
DIMINISHED SCALE

SCALES

STARTING ON 4TH STRING

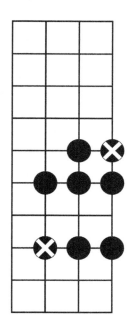
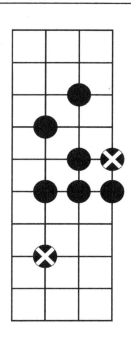
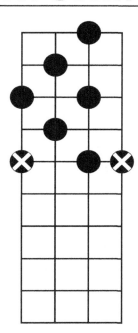

FIG.127 - LOCRIAN BEGINNING ON 4TH STRING

STARTING ON 3RD STRING

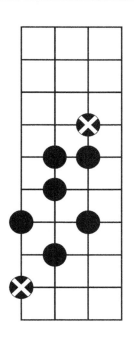
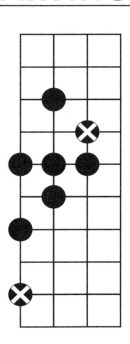
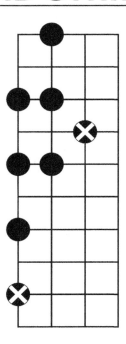

FIG.128 - LOCRIAN BEGINNING ON 3RD STRING

LINEAR 4TH STRING

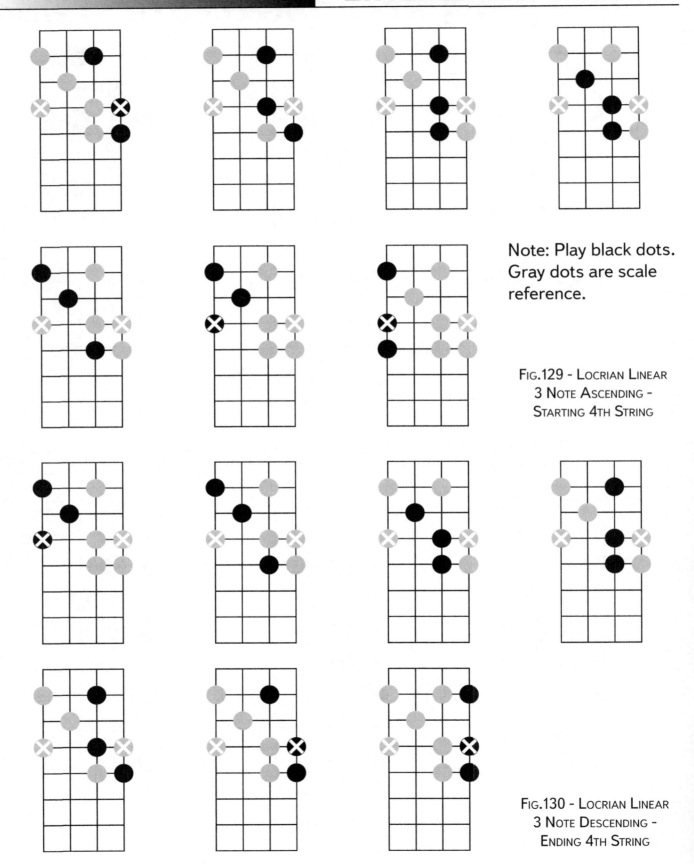

Note: Play black dots. Gray dots are scale reference.

Fig.129 - Locrian Linear 3 Note Ascending - Starting 4th String

Fig.130 - Locrian Linear 3 Note Descending - Ending 4th String

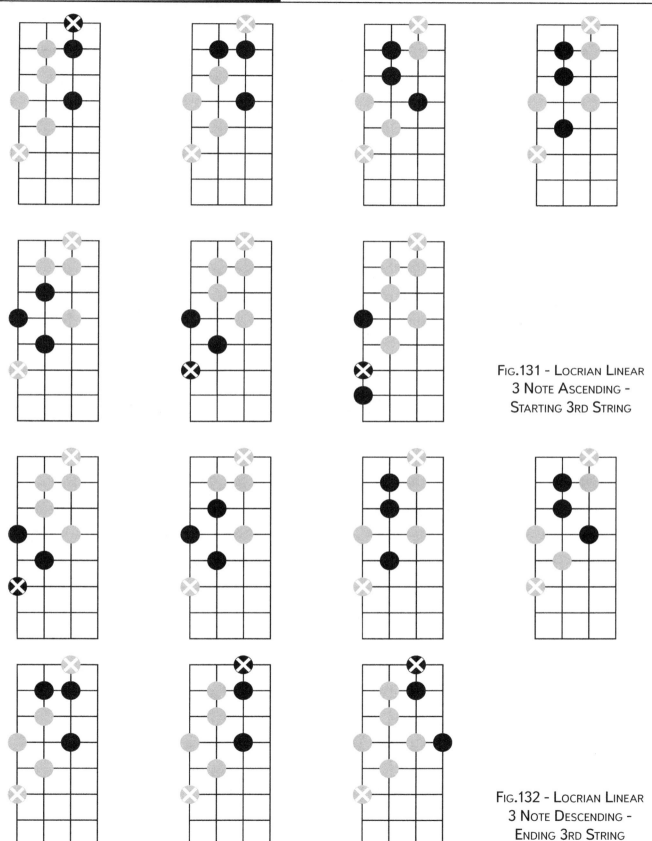

FIG.131 - LOCRIAN LINEAR
3 NOTE ASCENDING -
STARTING 3RD STRING

FIG.132 - LOCRIAN LINEAR
3 NOTE DESCENDING -
ENDING 3RD STRING

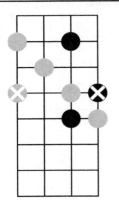
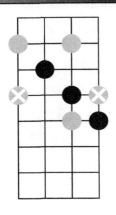
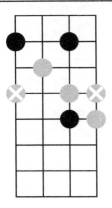
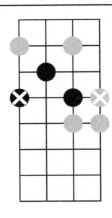

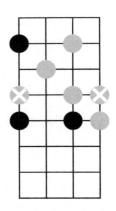
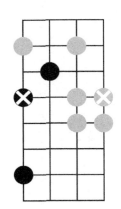
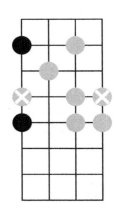

FIG.133 - LOCRIAN
3RDS ASCENDING -
STARTING 4TH STRING

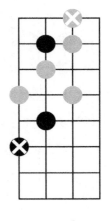
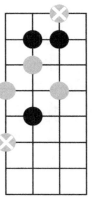
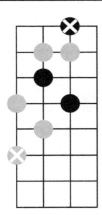

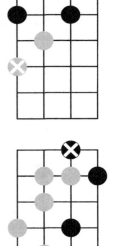
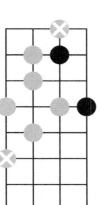

FIG.134 - LOCRIAN
3RDS DESCENDING -
ENDING 3RD STRING

MAJOR PENTATONIC

|||||||||||||||||||||||||||||||||||||||||||||||||||||||||||||||||

IN THIS UNIVERSE

Pentatonic scales are always made from 5 notes, as you may have guessed from their name. The major pentatonic is a subset of the notes of a major scale. Until now, all the scales you've seen have been made of 7 notes. Perhaps surprisingly, a scale made of only 5 notes is still extremely useful!

|||||||||||||||||||||||||||||||||||||||||||||||||||||||||||||||||

OVERVIEW

Spelling

Intervals	R	M2	M3	P5	M6	R
Example	C	D	E	G	A	C

FIG.135 - MAJOR PENTATONIC SPELLING

Common Style and Genre Use

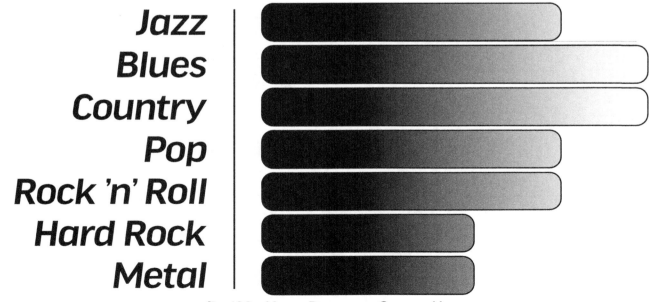

Jazz
Blues
Country
Pop
Rock 'n' Roll
Hard Rock
Metal

FIG.136 - MAJOR PENTATONIC COMMON USAGE

Chord Family

Containing a Major 2nd, 3rd, Perfect 5th and Major 6th makes the major pentatonic a great candidate for use with extended Major chords.

6 /9   13

FIG.137 - MAJOR PENTATONIC CHORD FAMILY

Scale Substitutions

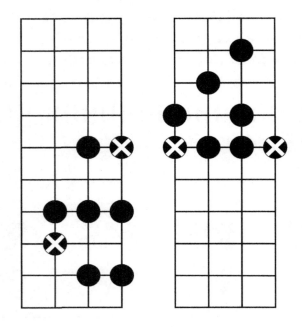

FIG.138 - IONIAN SCALE

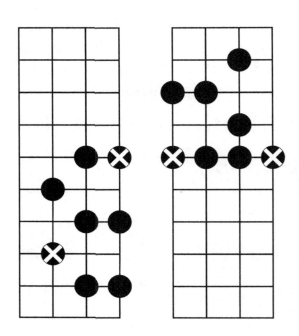

FIG.139 - MIXOLYDIAN SCALE

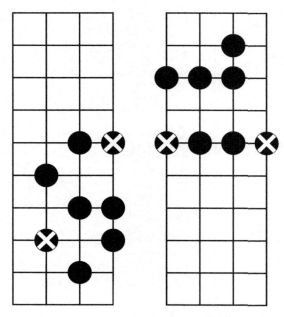

FIG.140 - DORIAN SCALE

SCALES

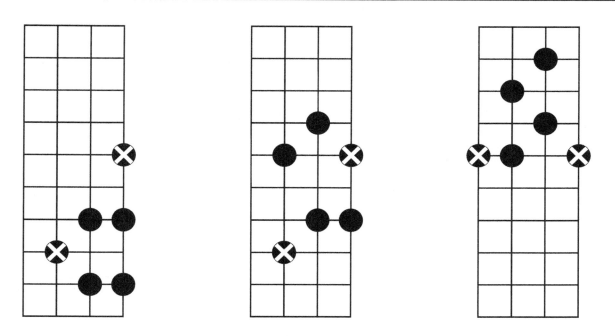

FIG.141 - MAJOR PENTATONIC BEGINNING ON 4TH STRING

STARTING ON 3RD STRING

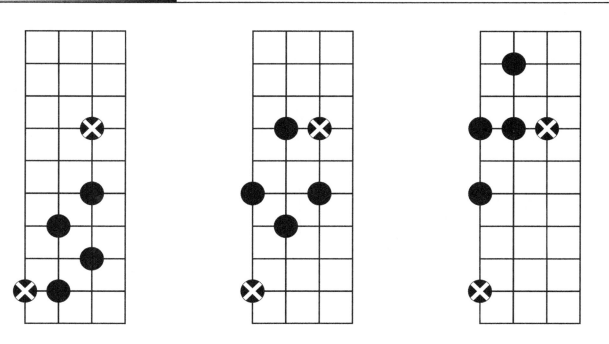

FIG.142 - MAJOR PENTATONIC BEGINNING ON 3RD STRING

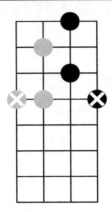
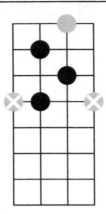
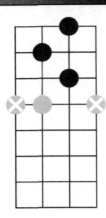
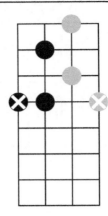

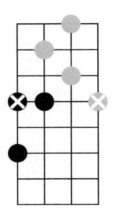

Note: Play black dots. Gray dots are scale reference.

FIG.143 - MAJOR PENTATONIC LINEAR 3 NOTE ASCENDING - STARTING 4TH STRING

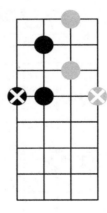
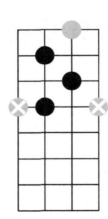
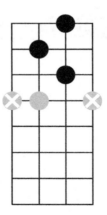
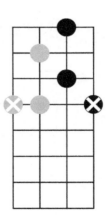

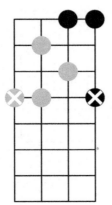

FIG.144 - MAJOR PENTATONIC LINEAR 3 NOTE DESCENDING - ENDING 4TH STRING

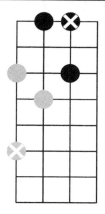

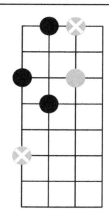
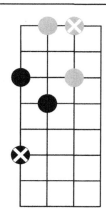

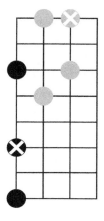

Fig.145 - Major Pentatonic Linear
3 Note Ascending -
Starting 3rd String

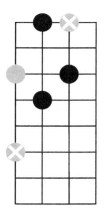
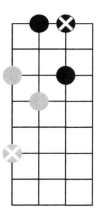

Fig.146 - Major Pentatonic Linear
3 Note Descending -
Ending 3rd String

MAJOR PENTATONIC 77

78 LEFT-HANDED BANJO SCALES INFINITY: A SEEING MUSIC METHOD BOOK

MINOR PENTATONIC

|||||||||||||||||||||||||||||||||||||||||||||||||||||||||||||||||||||||||

IN THIS UNIVERSE

Also made from just 5 notes, the minor pentatonic is a subset of the notes of the natural minor scale, also known as Aeolian. It is perhaps the most widely used scale in popular music today.

|||||||||||||||||||||||||||||||||||||||||||||||||||||||||||||||||||||||||

OVERVIEW

Spelling

Intervals	**R**	**m3**	**P4**	**P5**	**m7**	**R**
Example	C	E♭	F	G	B♭	C

FIG.147 - MINOR PENTATONIC SPELLING

Common Style and Genre Use

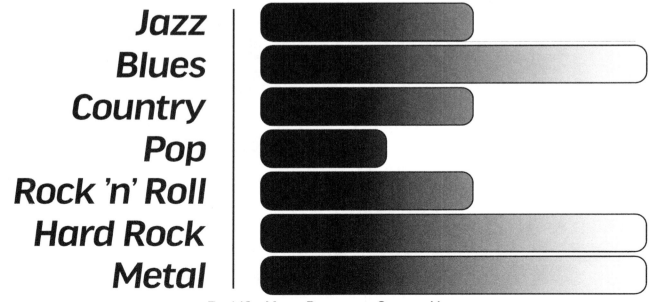

FIG.148 - MINOR PENTATONIC COMMON USAGE

Chord Family

Containing a minor 3rd and minor 7th, the minor pentatonic (or minor *pent*, to hip musicians) sounds terrific with a wide variety of chords.

min   min7   #9

FIG.149 - MAJOR PENTATONIC CHORD FAMILY

Scale Substitutions

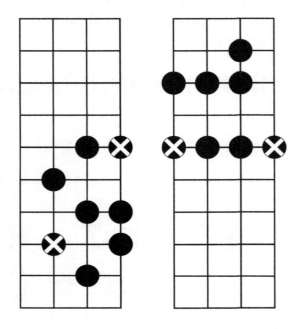

FIG.150 - DORIAN SCALE

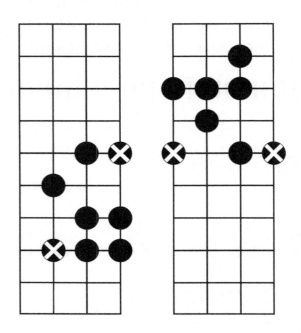

FIG.151 - AEOLIAN SCALE

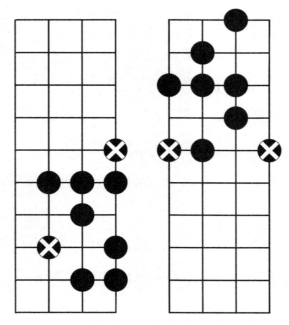

FIG.152 - HALF-WHOLE DIMINISHED SCALE

80 LEFT-HANDED BANJO SCALES INFINITY: A SEEING MUSIC METHOD BOOK

SCALES

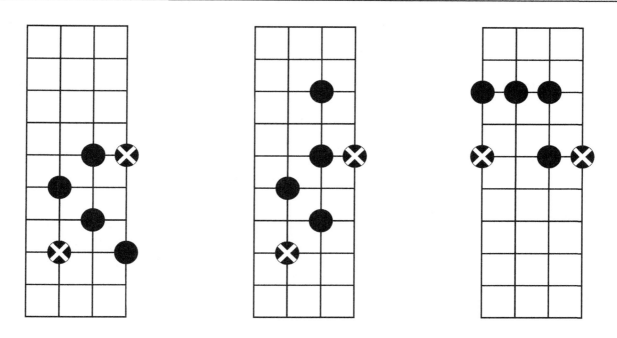

FIG.153 - MINOR PENTATONIC BEGINNING ON 4TH STRING

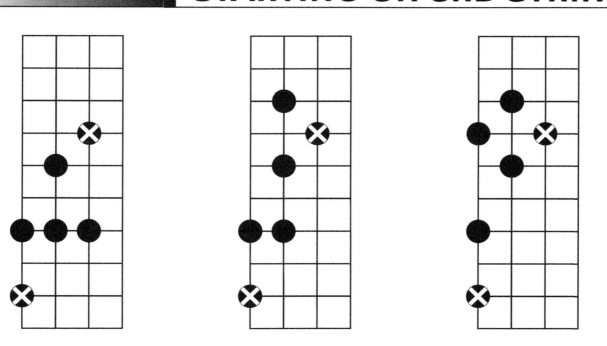

FIG.154 - MINOR PENTATONIC BEGINNING ON 3RD STRING

LINEAR 4TH STRING

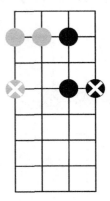 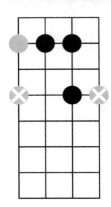 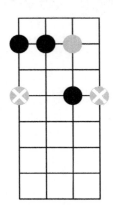 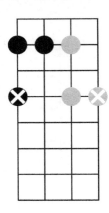

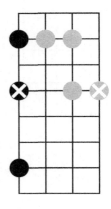

Note: Play black dots. Gray dots are scale reference.

FIG.155 - MINOR PENTATONIC LINEAR 3 NOTE ASCENDING - STARTING 4TH STRING

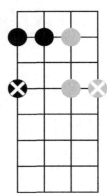 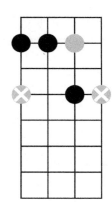 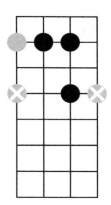 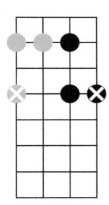

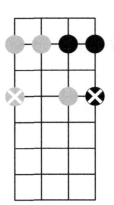

FIG.156 - MINOR PENTATONIC LINEAR 3 NOTE DESCENDING - ENDING 4TH STRING

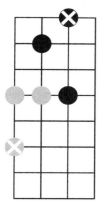 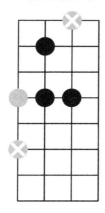 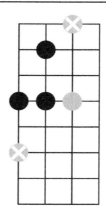 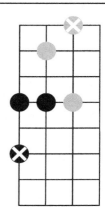

FIG.157 - MINOR PENTATONIC LINEAR
3 NOTE ASCENDING -
STARTING 3RD STRING

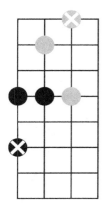 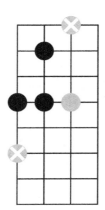 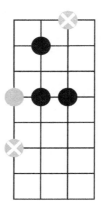 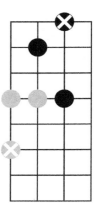

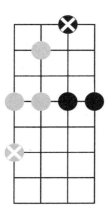

FIG.158 - MINOR PENTATONIC LINEAR
3 NOTE DESCENDING -
ENDING 3RD STRING

BLUES SCALE

IN THIS UNIVERSE

Closely related to the minor pentatonic, the blues scale adds one note, the flatted 5th or *tritone*. It's named for it's prevalence in Blues music.

OVERVIEW

Spelling

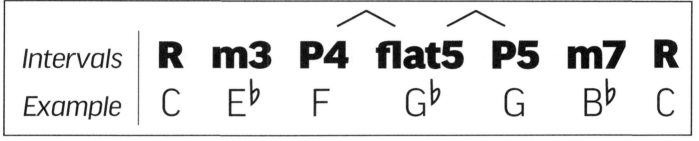

Intervals	R	m3	P4	flat5	P5	m7	R
Example	C	E♭	F	G♭	G	B♭	C

FIG.159 - BLUES SCALE SPELLING

Common Style and Genre Use

Jazz
Blues
Country
Pop
Rock 'n' Roll
Hard Rock
Metal

FIG.160 - BLUES SCALE COMMON USAGE

Chord Family

The blues scale can be viewed as a minor pentatonic with the addition of a flatted 5th. It is often used as a more colorful version of the minor pentatonic.

min   min7   #9   min7♭5

FIG.161 - BLUES SCALE CHORD FAMILY

Scale Substitutions

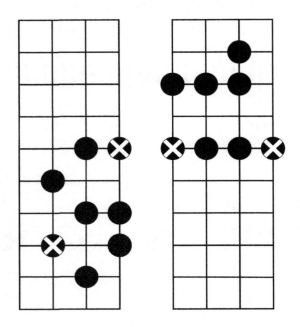

FIG.162 - DORIAN SCALE

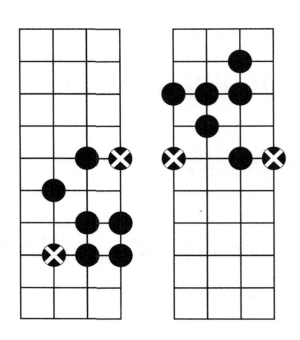

FIG.163 - AEOLIAN SCALE

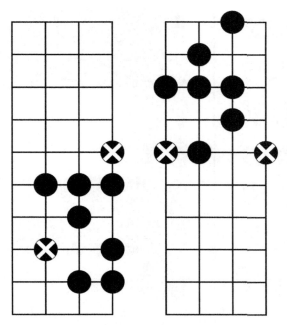

FIG.164 - HALF-WHOLE
DIMINISHED SCALE

86 LEFT-HANDED BANJO SCALES INFINITY: A SEEING MUSIC METHOD BOOK

SCALES

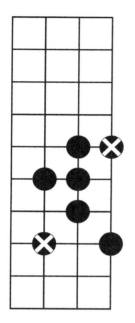 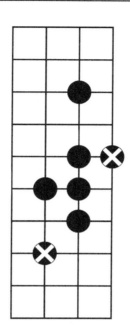 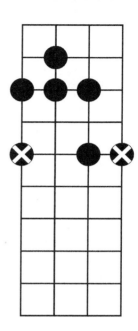

FIG.165 - BLUES SCALE BEGINNING ON 4TH STRING

STARTING ON 3RD STRING

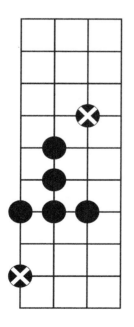 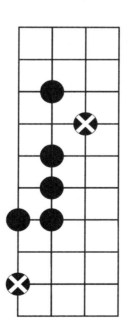 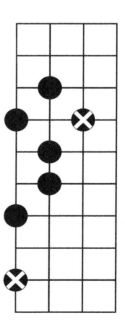

FIG.166 - BLUES SCALE BEGINNING ON 3RD STRING

LINEAR 4TH STRING

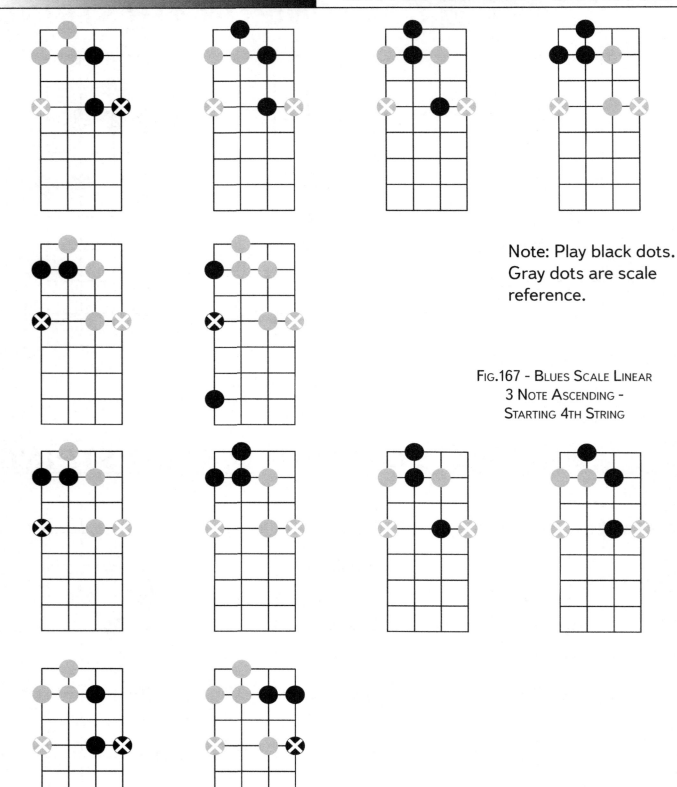

Note: Play black dots. Gray dots are scale reference.

Fig.167 - Blues Scale Linear 3 Note Ascending - Starting 4th String

Fig.168 - Blues Scale Linear 3 Note Descending - Ending 4th String

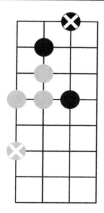
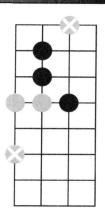
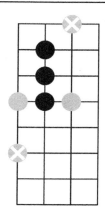
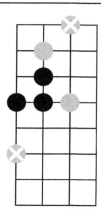

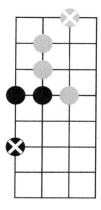

FIG.169 - BLUES SCALE LINEAR
3 NOTE ASCENDING -
STARTING 3RD STRING

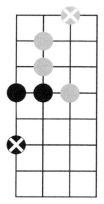
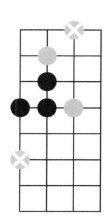

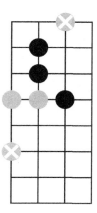

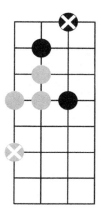
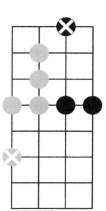

FIG.170 - BLUES SCALE LINEAR
3 NOTE DESCENDING -
ENDING 3RD STRING

90 LEFT-HANDED BANJO SCALES INFINITY: A SEEING MUSIC METHOD BOOK

WHOLE TONE

||||||||||||||||||||||||||||||||||||||||||||||||||||||||||||||||||||||||||||

IN THIS UNIVERSE

The whole tone scale is used primarily in Jazz music. Unlike modal scales, it is not a derivative of the Ionian scale. It is comprised entirely of whole step intervals, making it very unique.

||||||||||||||||||||||||||||||||||||||||||||||||||||||||||||||||||||||||||||

OVERVIEW

Spelling

Intervals	**R**	**M2**	**M3**	**flat5**	**#5**	**m7**	**R**
Example	C	D	E	G♭	G♯	B♭	C

FIG.171 - WHOLE TONE SPELLING

Common Style and Genre Use

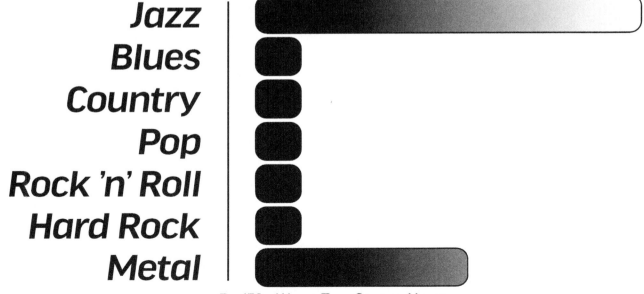

FIG.172 - WHOLE TONE COMMON USAGE

Chord Family

The whole tone scale holds the major 3rd, flat 5th, sharp 5th and minor 7th intervals, making it well suited for augmented chords and altered dominant flavors.

Aug   7♭5   7♯5

FIG.173 - WHOLE TONE CHORD FAMILY

Scale Substitutions

No common substitutions

SCALES

STARTING ON 4TH STRING

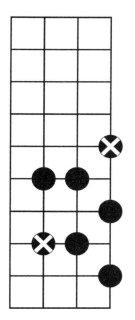 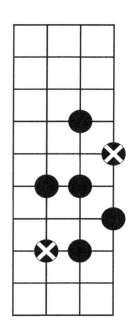 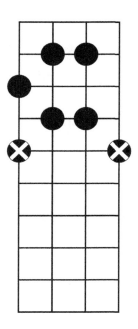

FIG.174 - WHOLE TONE BEGINNING ON 4TH STRING

STARTING ON 3RD STRING

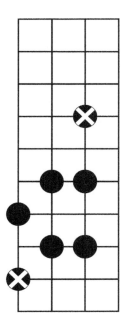 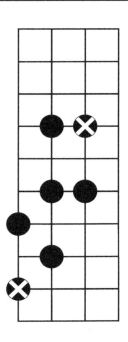 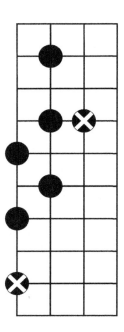

FIG.175 - WHOLE TONE BEGINNING ON 3RD STRING

LINEAR 4TH STRING

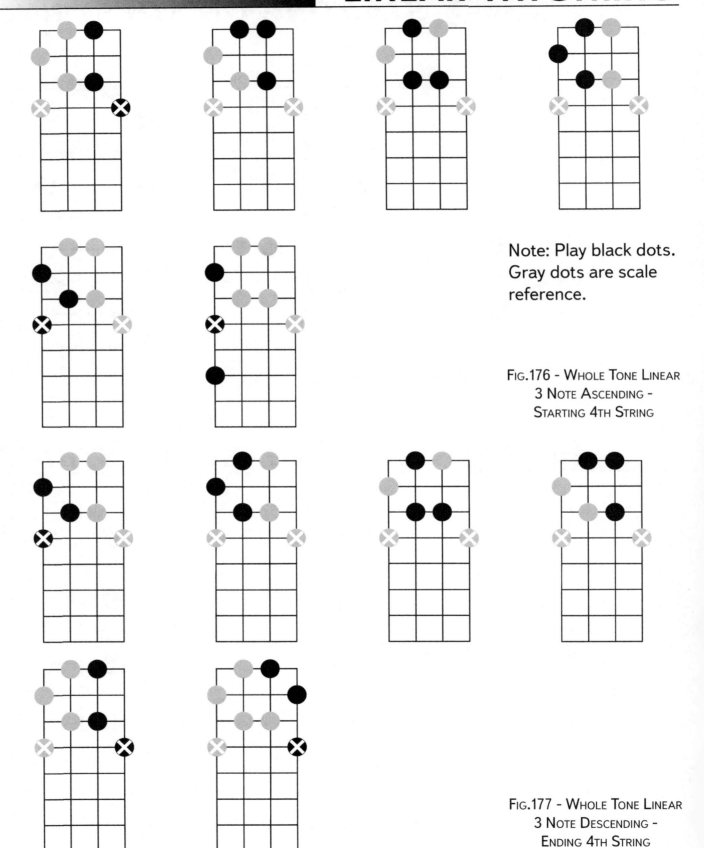

Note: Play black dots. Gray dots are scale reference.

FIG.176 - WHOLE TONE LINEAR 3 NOTE ASCENDING - STARTING 4TH STRING

FIG.177 - WHOLE TONE LINEAR 3 NOTE DESCENDING - ENDING 4TH STRING

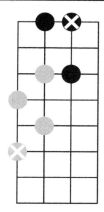
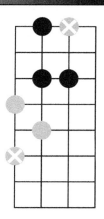
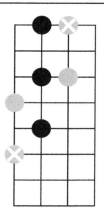
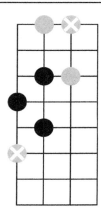

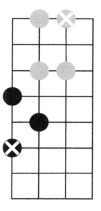
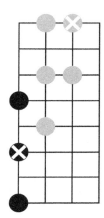

FIG.178 - WHOLE TONE LINEAR
3 NOTE ASCENDING -
STARTING 3RD STRING

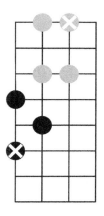
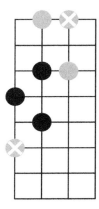
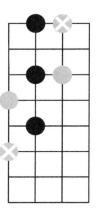
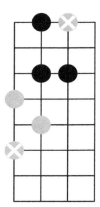

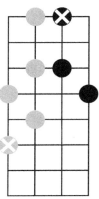

FIG.179 - WHOLE TONE LINEAR
3 NOTE DESCENDING -
ENDING 3RD STRING

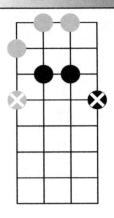 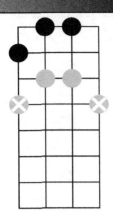 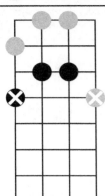 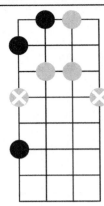

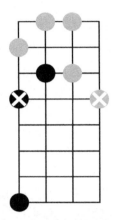

FIG.180 - WHOLE TONE
3RDS ASCENDING -
STARTING 4TH STRING

3RDS DESCENDING

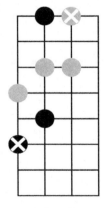 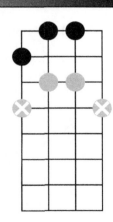 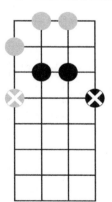 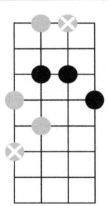

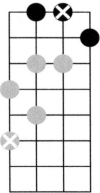

FIG.181 - WHOLE TONE
3RDS DESCENDING -
ENDING 3RD STRING

HALF/WHOLE DIMINISHED

IN THIS UNIVERSE

The half/whole diminished scale is another very unique scale, made of repetitive intervals. The repeating pattern is one of a half-step followed by a whole step. It is known by a few names, including "half-diminished" and "octatonic".

OVERVIEW

Spelling

Intervals	R	m2	m3	M3	#4	P5	M6	m7	R
Example	C	D♭	E♭	E	F♯	G	A	B♭	C

FIG.182 - HALF/WHOLE DIMINISHED SPELLING

Common Style and Genre Use

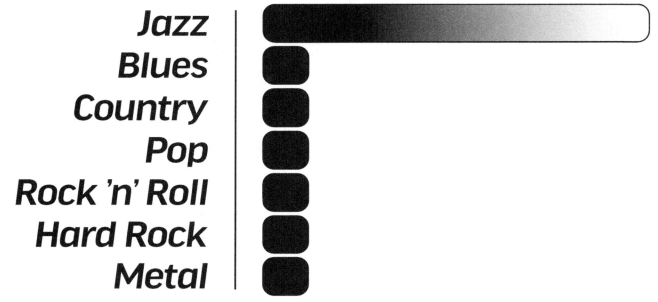

- Jazz
- Blues
- Country
- Pop
- Rock 'n' Roll
- Hard Rock
- Metal

FIG.183 - HALF/WHOLE DIMINISHED COMMON USAGE

Chord Family

A favorite with jazz musicians, it is sometimes said the half/whole diminished scale has it all. Holding a minor 2nd, 3rd and 7th as well as the major 3rd and sharp 4th/flatted 5th, the half/whole diminished scale is a great match for many altered dominant flavors.

7   ♭9   ♯9   dim   Ø7

FIG.184 - HALF/WHOLE DIMINISHED CHORD FAMILY

Scale Substitutions

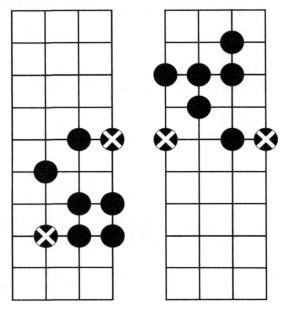

FIG.185 - AEOLIAN SCALE

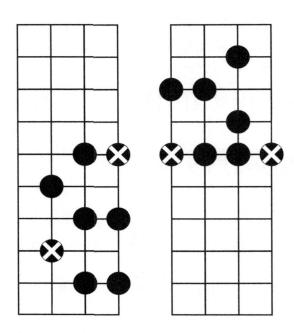

FIG.186 - MIXOLYDIAN SCALE

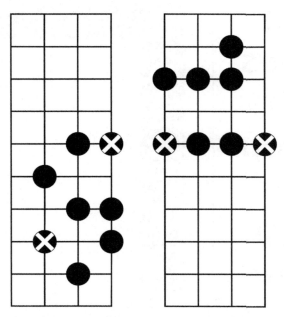

FIG.187 - DORIAN SCALE

SCALES

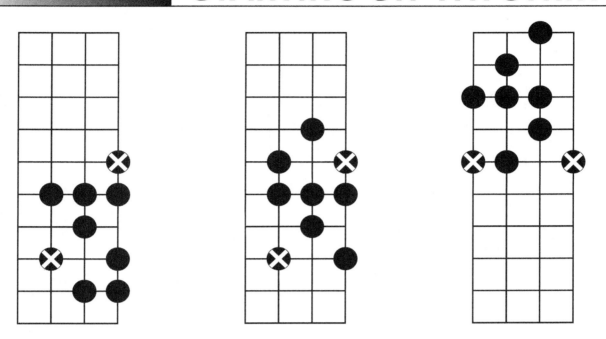

FIG.188 - HALF/WHOLE DIMINISHED BEGINNING ON 4TH STRING

STARTING ON 3RD STRING

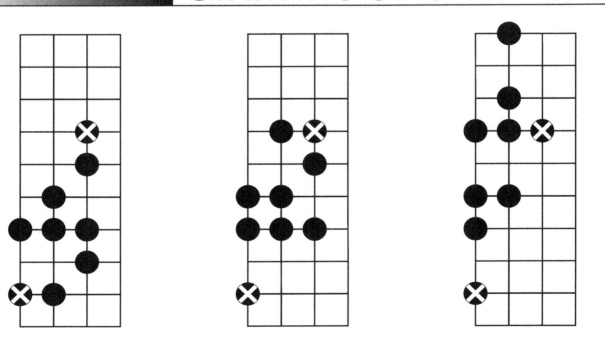

FIG.189 - HALF/WHOLE DIMINISHED BEGINNING ON 3RD STRING

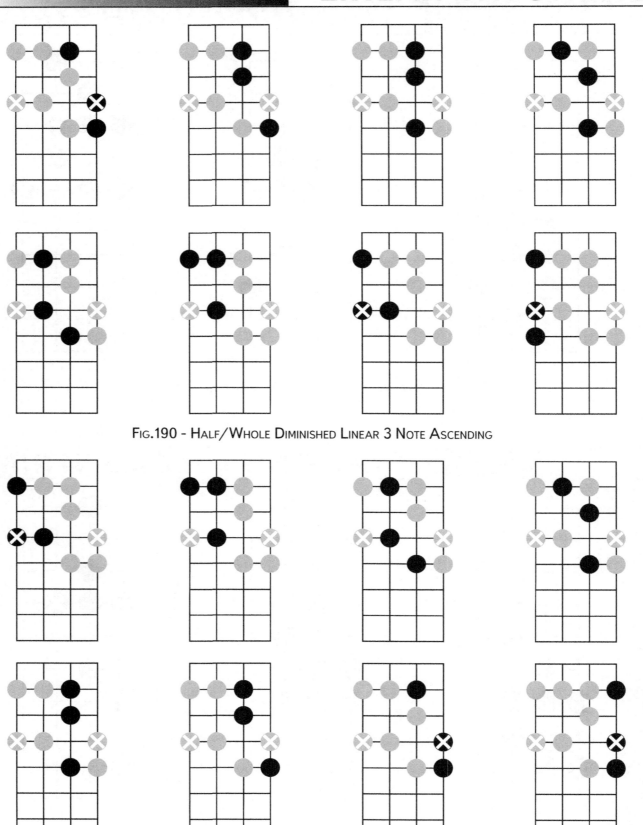

FIG.190 - HALF/WHOLE DIMINISHED LINEAR 3 NOTE ASCENDING

FIG.191 - HALF/WHOLE DIMINISHED LINEAR 3 NOTE DESCENDING

100 LEFT-HANDED BANJO SCALES INFINITY: A SEEING MUSIC METHOD BOOK

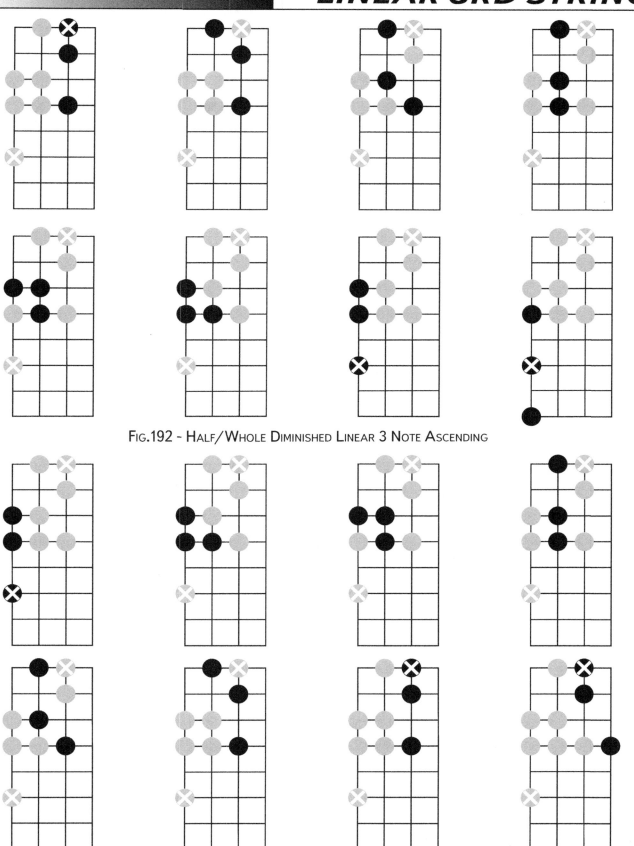

FIG.192 - HALF/WHOLE DIMINISHED LINEAR 3 NOTE ASCENDING

FIG.193 - HALF/WHOLE DIMINISHED LINEAR 3 NOTE DESCENDING

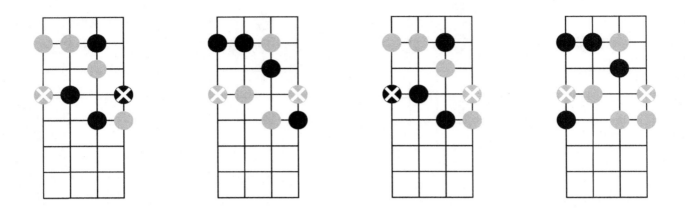

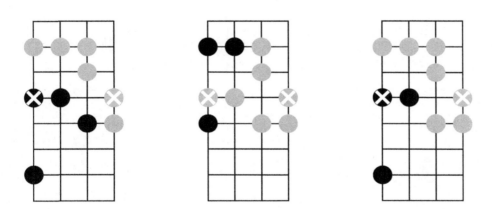

FIG.194 - HALF/WHOLE DIMINISHED 3RDS ASCENDING

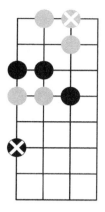 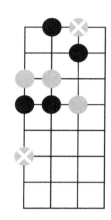 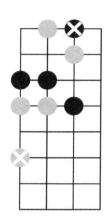 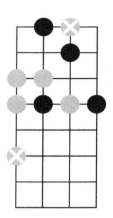

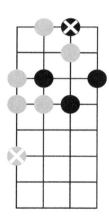 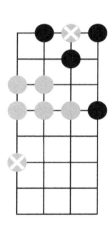

FIG.195 - HALF/WHOLE DIMINISHED 3RDS DESCENDING

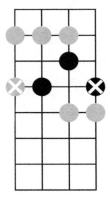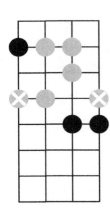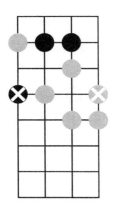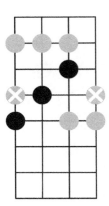

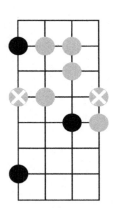

FIG.196 - HALF/WHOLE DIMINISHED INVERTED TRIADS ASCENDING

MELODIC MINOR

IIIIIIIIIIIIIIIIIIIIIIIIIIIIIIIIIIIIIIIIIIIIIIIIIIIIIIIIIIIIIIIIIIIIIIIIIIIIIIIIIIII

IN THIS UNIVERSE

Priniciply used in Classical music, melodic minor is rarely heard in more modern music. It is rather unique in that it takes one form ascending, and another form when descending.

IIIIIIIIIIIIIIIIIIIIIIIIIIIIIIIIIIIIIIIIIIIIIIIIIIIIIIIIIIIIIIIIIIIIIIIIIIIIIIIIIIII

OVERVIEW

Spelling

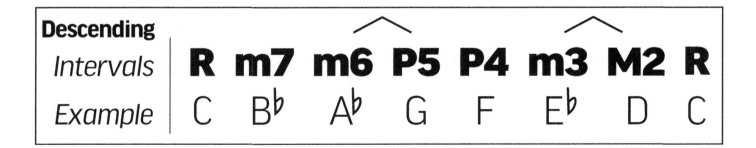

Ascending								
Intervals	**R**	**M2**	**m3**	**P4**	**P5**	**M6**	**M7**	**R**
Example	C	D	E♭	F	G	A	B	C

Descending								
Intervals	**R**	**m7**	**m6**	**P5**	**P4**	**m3**	**M2**	**R**
Example	C	B♭	A♭	G	F	E♭	D	C

FIG.197 - MELODIC MINOR SPELLING

Common Style and Genre Use

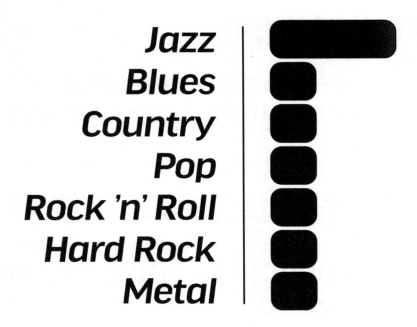

Jazz
Blues
Country
Pop
Rock 'n' Roll
Hard Rock
Metal

FIG.198 - MELODIC MINOR COMMON USAGE

Chord Family

Although not very similar to natural minor, melodic minor might be used anywhere natural minor would be an obvious choice.

$$min \qquad min7 \qquad min9 \qquad min^{\triangle}7$$

FIG.199 - MELODIC MINOR CHORD FAMILY

Scale Substitutions

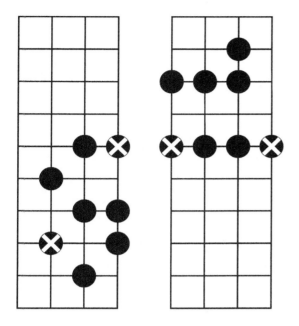

FIG.200 - DORIAN SCALE

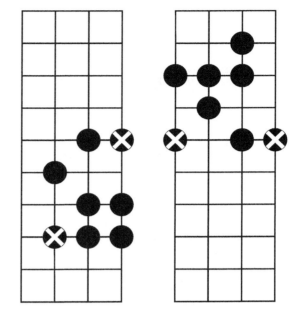

FIG.201 - AEOLIAN SCALE

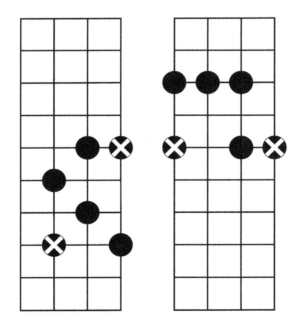

FIG.202 - MINOR PENTATONIC

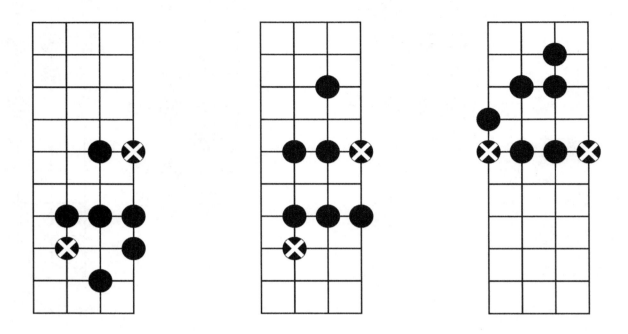

FIG.203 - MELODIC MINOR BEGINNING ON 4TH STRING - ASCENDING

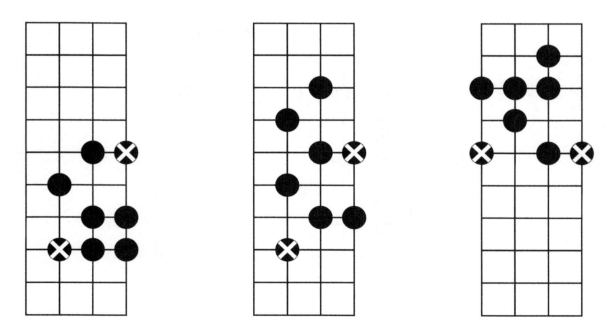

FIG.204 - MELODIC MINOR ENDING ON 4TH STRING - DESCENDING

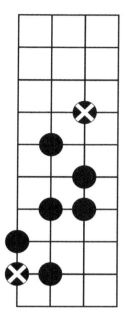 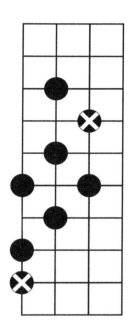 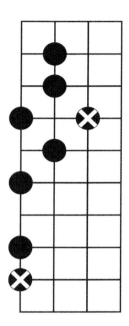

FIG.205 - MELODIC MINOR BEGINNING ON 3RD STRING - ASCENDING

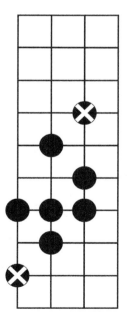 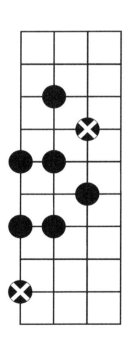 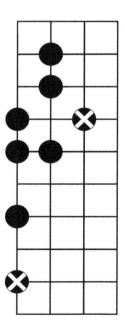

FIG.206 - MELODIC MINOR ENDING ON 3RD STRING - DESCENDING

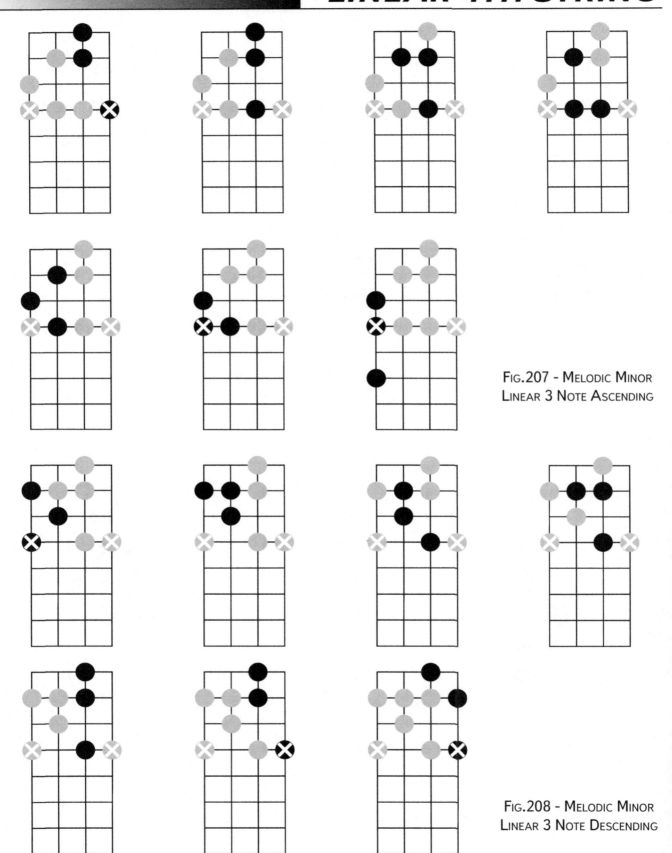

Fig.207 - Melodic Minor
Linear 3 Note Ascending

Fig.208 - Melodic Minor
Linear 3 Note Descending

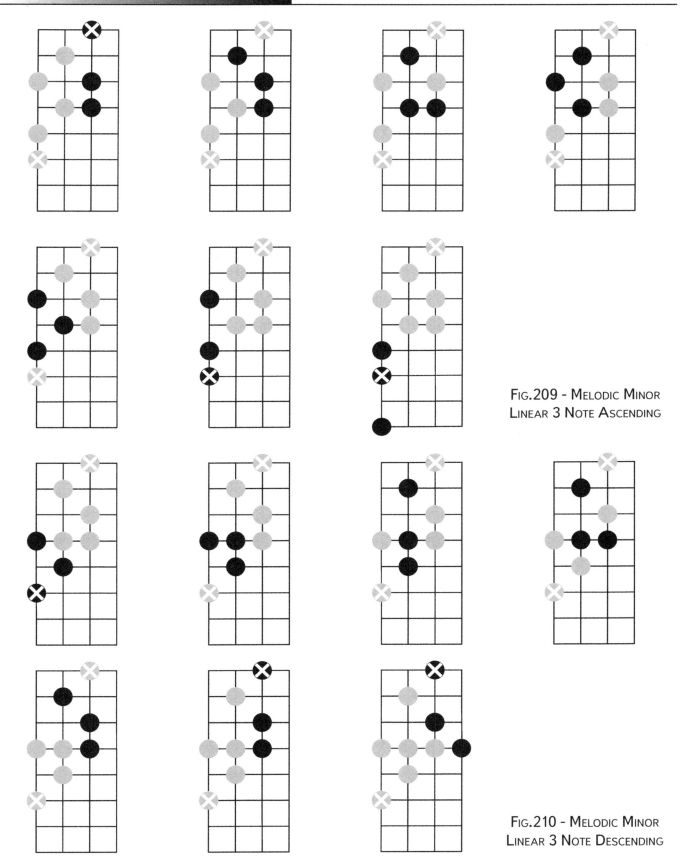

FIG.209 - MELODIC MINOR
LINEAR 3 NOTE ASCENDING

FIG.210 - MELODIC MINOR
LINEAR 3 NOTE DESCENDING

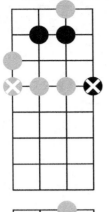
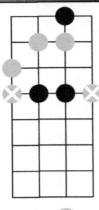
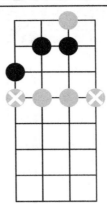
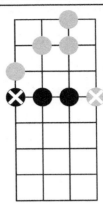

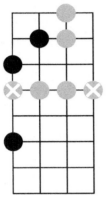
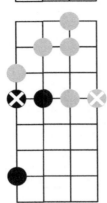

FIG.211 - MELODIC MINOR
3RDS ASCENDING

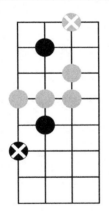
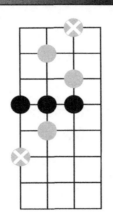
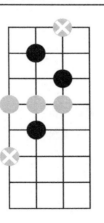
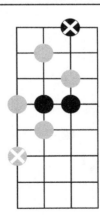

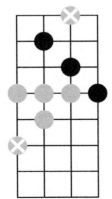
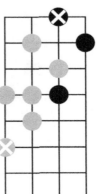
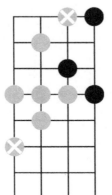

FIG.212 - MELODIC MINOR
3RDS DESCENDING

LEFT-HANDED
BANJO SCALES
INFINITY

114 LEFT-HANDED BANJO SCALES INFINITY: A SEEING MUSIC METHOD BOOK

HARMONIC MINOR

||||||||||||||||||||||||||||||||||||||||||||||||||||||||||||||||||||

IN THIS UNIVERSE

Harmonic minor has a unique flavor that is associated with Eastern melody. Owing to it's minor 3rd but major 7th contributions, it has a harmonic signature that is instantly identifiable.

||||||||||||||||||||||||||||||||||||||||||||||||||||||||||||||||||||

OVERVIEW

Spelling

Intervals	R	M2	m3	P4	P5	m6	M7	R
Example	C	D	E♭	F	G	A♭	B	C

FIG.213 - HARMONIC MINOR SPELLING

Common Style and Genre Use

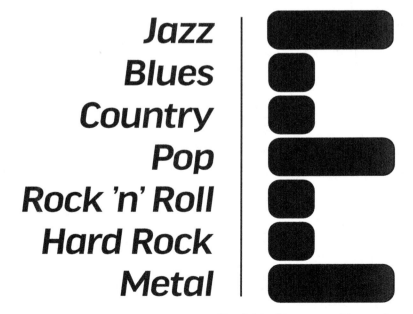

Jazz
Blues
Country
Pop
Rock 'n' Roll
Hard Rock
Metal

FIG.214 - HARMONIC MINOR COMMON USAGE

Chord Family

While the minor (Major 7th) chord is the natural choice, adventurous musicians might use harmonic minor with either major or minor chords.

min$^{\triangle}$7

Maj7   Maj9   min7   min9

FIG.215 - HARMONIC MINOR CHORD FAMILY

Scale Substitutions

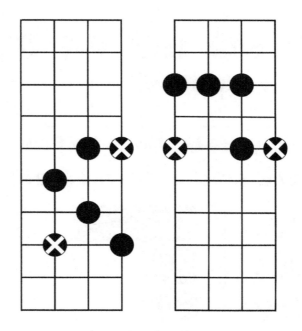

FIG.216 - MINOR PENTATONIC SCALE

SCALES

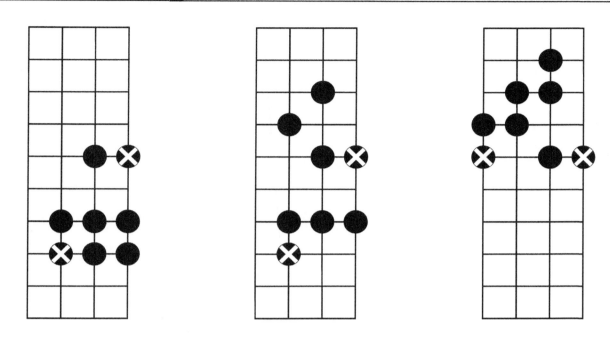

FIG.217 - HARMONIC MINOR BEGINNING ON 4TH STRING

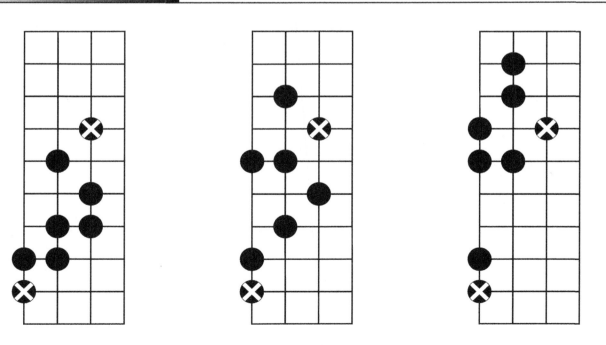

FIG.218 - HARMONIC MINOR BEGINNING ON 3RD STRING

LINEAR 4TH STRING

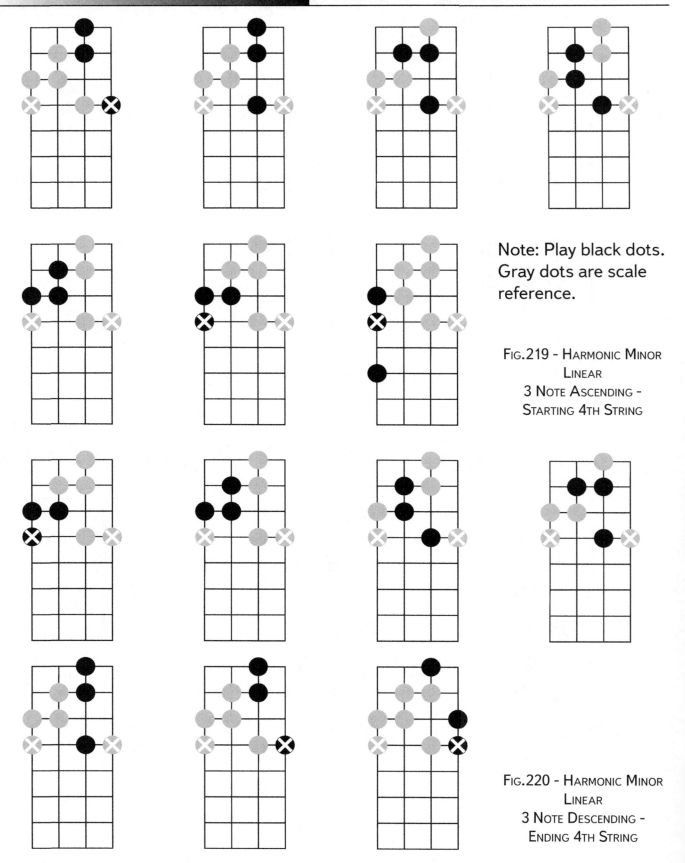

Note: Play black dots. Gray dots are scale reference.

FIG.219 - HARMONIC MINOR
LINEAR
3 NOTE ASCENDING -
STARTING 4TH STRING

FIG.220 - HARMONIC MINOR
LINEAR
3 NOTE DESCENDING -
ENDING 4TH STRING

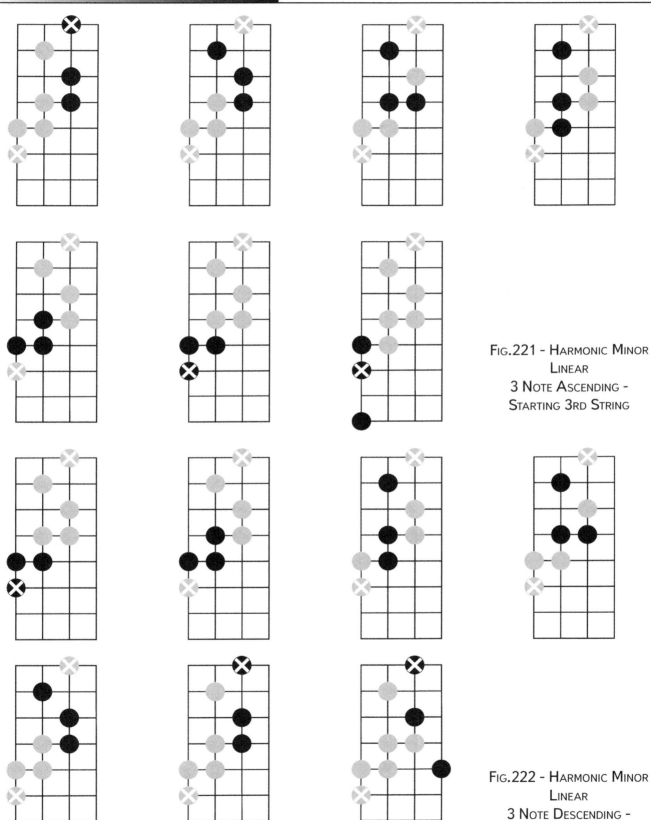

FIG.221 - HARMONIC MINOR
LINEAR
3 NOTE ASCENDING -
STARTING 3RD STRING

FIG.222 - HARMONIC MINOR
LINEAR
3 NOTE DESCENDING -
ENDING 3RD STRING

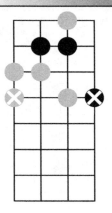
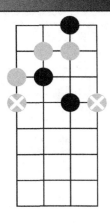
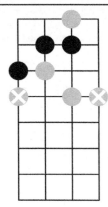
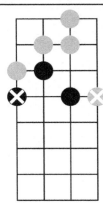

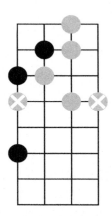
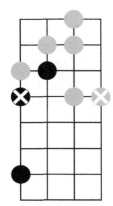
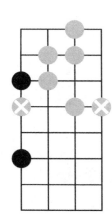

FIG.223 - HARMONIC MINOR 3RDS ASCENDING - STARTING 4TH STRING

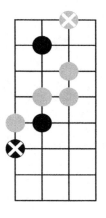

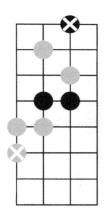

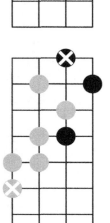
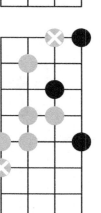
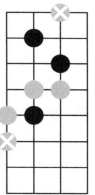

FIG.224 - HARMONIC MINOR 3RDS DESCENDING - ENDING 3RD STRING

CHROMATIC

||||||||||||||||||||||||||||||||||||||||||||||||||||||||||||||||

IN THIS UNIVERSE

The chromatic scale contains every note: natural, flat and sharp. All intervals are half-steps and it is more commonly heard in jazz, classical and cinematic music.

||||||||||||||||||||||||||||||||||||||||||||||||||||||||||||||||

OVERVIEW

Spelling

	∧	∧	∧	∧	∧	∧	∧	∧	∧	∧	∧	∧	∧
Intervals	R	m2	M2	m3	M3	P4	flat5	P5	m6	M6	m7	M7	R
Example	C	D$^\flat$	D	E$^\flat$	E	F	G$^\flat$	G	A$^\flat$	A	B$^\flat$	B	C

FIG.225 - IONIAN SPELLING

Common Style and Genre Use

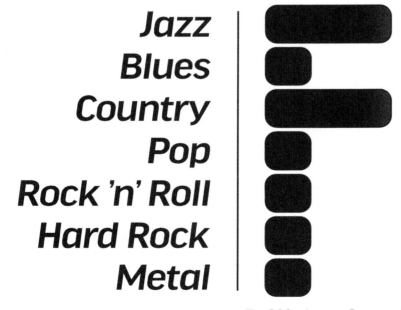

Jazz
Blues
Country
Pop
Rock 'n' Roll
Hard Rock
Metal

FIG.226 - IONIAN COMMON USAGE

Chord Family

The chromatic scale, containing every note, is not closely associated with any chords. Containing every note of any chord, it doesn't have an affinity for any chord set.

Scale Substitutions

Owing to the fact that this scale is not closely associated with any specific chords, there are no occasions in which to substitute any other scale for the chromatic scale. Because of this, it substitutes *in place of* other scales, but other scales do not substitute for it.

As an example, a progression of chords might be C Major, A Minor and G Major. A musician might opt to improvise with the chromatic chord over any of these chords as a departure from more standard diatonic chord/scale choices.

SCALES

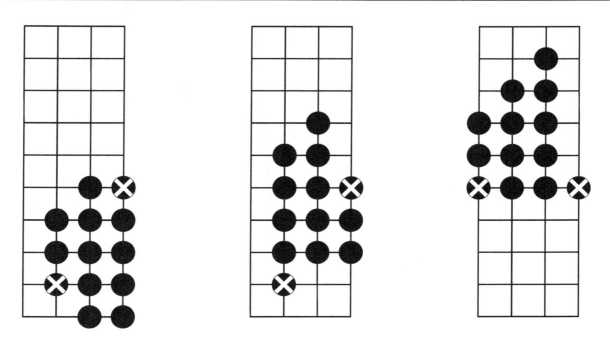

FIG.227 - CHROMATIC SCALE BEGINNING ON 4TH STRING

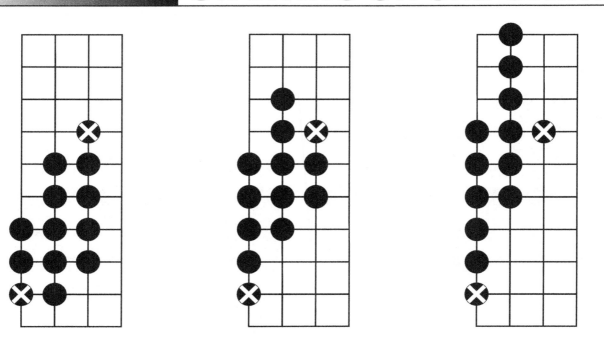

FIG.228 - CHROMATIC SCALE BEGINNING ON 3RD STRING

You've got big ideas.
Keep them organized.
Over 100 Pages of Clean Single-Staff Paper
Clean Design and Easy-to-Use Matte Finish
Saves Time and Clutter in Your Music Space
Includes a Fill-In Table of Contents to Keep Track of Your Compositions
SEEING MUSIC
METHOD BOOKS
Lots of Clean Single-Staff Sheets to Organize Your Music
JUST
BLANK
STAFF PAPER
ANDY SCHNEIDER
ALL LEVELS

YOU'VE EXPLORED THE UNIVERSE

Time to congratulate yourself on all you've learned!

- Modes of major scales

- How to create mini-melodies from linear or triadic movement

- How to re-order and re-invent those mini-melodies

- Several types of minor scales

- Scales not derivative of the major scale

- Relationships between scales and chord families

- Many substitutions for scales

Keep in mind, this book cannot begin to capture every scale in the world. You may wish to explore even more exotic scales, such as Gypsy scales or the many different tunings and scales used across the world by other cultures. Additionally, just as you saw how to use the modes of the major scale (Ionian), you might explore the modes of the other scales used in this book. How about the mode starting on the 5th degree of harmonic minor? How about the mode starting on the 2nd degree of half/whole diminished? Why not re-write each exercise starting not from the 4th string, but from the 3rd!

Infinity can be found within your own mind. Any time you're feeling confined, use your creativity to push the bounds of your music.

ASSIGNMENT

Today's Assignment

Keep learning! You're well on your way to total banjo and musical knowledge!

There are several books in the *Seeing Music* family you may find interesting to develop your knowledge and skill. *Seeing Music* books put you inside the mind of professional string instrumentalists everywhere who organize their vast knowledge by very simple visual means. Our books give you the tools to continue teaching yourself, to be able to play anything, anytime.

Keep on makin' music, musician!

CHORD AND MODE REFERENCE

Chords - Major

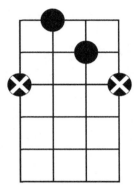

FIG.229 - MAJOR CHORD

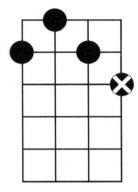

FIG.230 - MAJOR 7

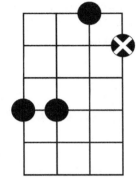

FIG.231 - MAJOR 9

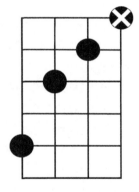

FIG.232 - MAJOR 7 SHARP 11

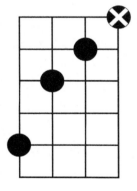

FIG.233 - MAJOR 7 FLAT 5

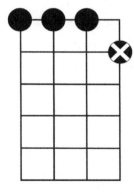

FIG.234 - MAJOR 7 SHARP 5

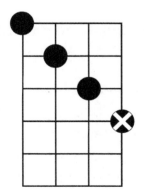

FIG.235 - MAJOR 13

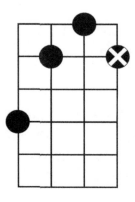

FIG.236 - 6/9

126 LEFT-HANDED BANJO SCALES INFINITY: A SEEING MUSIC METHOD BOOK

Chords - Minor

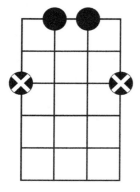

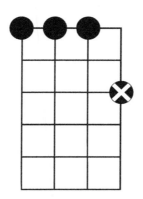

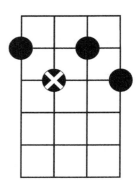

FIG.237 - MINOR CHORD   FIG.238 - MINOR 7   FIG.239 - MINOR 9

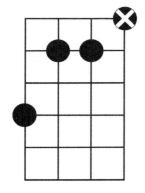

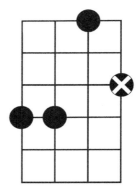

FIG.240 - MINOR 7 FLAT 5   FIG.241 - MINOR 7 FLAT 9

Note: In each diagram, the dot with the "X" denotes the root of the chord.

Chords - Dominant

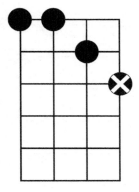

FIG.242 - 7TH CHORD

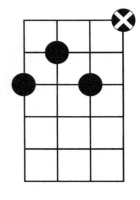

FIG.243 - 9TH CHORD

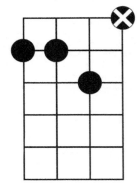

FIG.244 - 7 FLAT 9

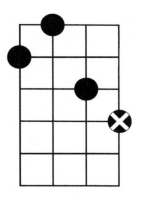

FIG.245 - 7 FLAT 5

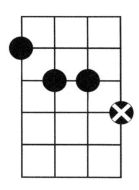

FIG.246 - 7 SHARP 5

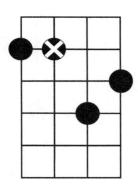

FIG.247 - 7 SHARP 9

Chords - Augmented and Diminished

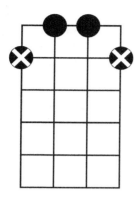

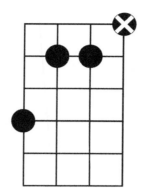

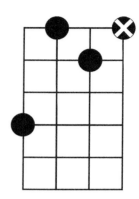

FIG.248 - AUGMENTED CHORD   FIG.249 - HALF-DIMINISHED CHORD   FIG.250 - FULL-DIMINISHED CHORD

Scales - Modes

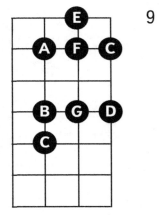

FIG.251 - C IONIAN

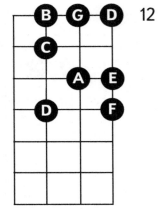

FIG.252 - D DORIAN

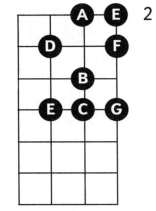

FIG.253 - E PHYRGIAN

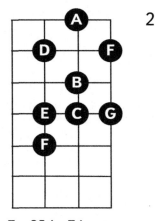

FIG.254 - F LYDIAN

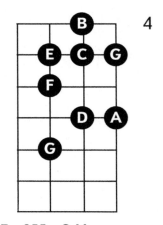

FIG.255 - G MIXOLYDIAN

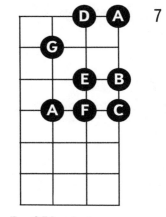

FIG.256 - A AEOLIAN

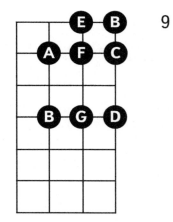

FIG.257 - B LOCRIAN

Printed in Great Britain
by Amazon

36549059R00073